No Extraordinary Power

Prayer,
Stillness
and Activism

"A Christian should be
without fear — happy and
always in trouble!"

To Ellen, with thanks for her
inspiration, love and companionship
through so many adventures together.

About the author

Helen Steven's journey in prayer and activism starts in Scotland. She is a graduate of Glasgow University and taught history in Glasgow for seven years. In 1972 she went to Vietnam as part of a Quaker project working in orphanages in Saigon, along with Ellen Moxley, who is now Helen's lifelong partner. These two years were a life changing experience and committed Helen to working for peace.

Brought up in the Church of Scotland, Helen was inspired by the way Quakers put their faith into practical action, and she became a member of the Quakers (the Religious Society of Friends) in 1976.

In 1979 Helen was employed by the Iona Community as their justice and peace worker, and, inspired by the commitment to social action of the Iona Community, she became a member of the Community in 1981. Supported by the Iona Community and Quaker Peace and Service, Helen and Ellen started Peace House, a residential centre in central Scotland. Twelve years and 10,000 guests later they left Peace House, and Helen founded the Scottish Centre for Nonviolence in Dunblane.

Helen's work for peace has taken her to NATO headquarters in Brussels, to many international conferences, to demonstrations at Faslane naval base, and occasionally to prison. In 2004 she and Ellen were awarded the Gandhi International Peace Prize.

Helen Steven

No Extraordinary Power

Prayer,
Stillness
and Activism

 Quaker Books   Swarthmore Lecture 2005

First published 1 August 2005 by Quaker Books
Friends House, 173 Euston Road, London NW1 2BJ
www.quaker.org.uk

ISBN 0 85245 379 5

Cover and text design Golden Cockerel Press Ltd, London.

Cover image Seattle, 1999, adapted from a video by Ricarda
Steinbrecher. © Ricarda Steinbrecher.

The Swarthmore Lecture

The Swarthmore Lectureship was established by the Woodbrooke Extension Committee at a meeting held 9 December 1907: the minute of the Committee providing for an "annual lecture on some subject relating to the message and work of the Society of Friends". The name Swarthmore was chosen in memory of the home of Margaret Fox, which was always open to the earnest seeker after Truth, and from which loving words of sympathy and substantial material help were sent to fellow workers.

The lectureship has a twofold purpose: first, to interpret to the members of the Society of Friends their message and mission; and second, to bring before the public the spirit, aims and fundamental principles of Friends. The lecturers alone are responsible for any opinions expressed.

The lectureship provides both for the publication of a book and for the delivery of a lecture, the latter usually at the time of Britain Yearly Meeting of the Society of Friends. A lecture related to the present book was delivered at Yearly Meeting in York on the evening of 1 August 2005.

The Swarthmore Lecture Committee can be contacted via the Clerk, c/o Woodbrooke Quaker Study Centre, 1046 Bristol Road, Selly Oak, Birmingham B29 6LJ.

Acknowledgments

"Iona Community Vision and Goals" (Appendix 1) © Iona
    Community, 2005, with special thanks to Kathy Galloway for
    latest available text at time of going to press
"We believe that God is present" affirmation © Iona Community,
    from *The Iona Abbey Worship Book*, 2001, Wild Goose
    Publications, Glasgow G2 3DH. www.ionabooks.com
"Take us outside, O Christ", from a prayer by George MacLeod,
    © Iona Community, from *The Iona Abbey Worship Book*, 2001,
    Wild Goose Publications, Glasgow G2 3DH. www.ionabooks.com
"Spirit of the Living God" © Iona Community, from *The Iona Abbey
    Worship Book*, 2001, Wild Goose Publications, Glasgow G2 3DH.
    www.ionabooks.com
The lines from "Natural Resources". Copyright © 2002 by Adrienne
    Rich. Copyright © 1978 by W.W. Norton & Company, Inc, from
    The Facto of a Doorframe: Selected Poems 1950–2001 by Adrienne
    Rich. Used by permission of the author and W.W. Norton &
    Company, Inc.
Excerpt "I consider a tree . . ." by Martin Buber. Reprinted with
    the permission of Simon & Schuster Adult Publishing Group,
    from *I and Thou* by Martin Buber, translated by Ronald Gregor
    Smith. Copyright © 1958 by Charles Scribner's Sons. By kind
    permission of Continuum.
Extract from *God of Surprises* © Gerard Hughes 1987, by permission
    of Darton, Longman & Todd Ltd.
Poem: "You can't stop that wind you can't kill that fire" in CND
    leaflet, World Council of Churches, reproduced with permission.

Contents

Preface   9

Introduction   11

Part One: Growing into Prayer
Early Years   15
A Praying Community   18
Experiments with Prayer   21
New Encounters   25
Some Awkward Questions   28

Part Two: Aspects of Prayer
The Everlasting Arms: Prayer as Upholding   33
Finding a Way: Prayer as Guidance and Discernment   36
Leaving the Comfort Zone: Prayer as Challenge   39
Dogged Persistence: Prayer as Importuning God   45
Ask for What you Need: Prayer as Petition   48
Breaking Free: Prayer as Repentance   54
A Burning in the Bones: Prayer as Resistance   58
A Precious Habitation: Prayer as a Way of Being   64

Part Three: Bedrock of Faith
A Cupboard of Delights   71
Ground of Our Being or Ancient of Days?   71
Reaching Beyond Ourselves   78
Reweaving the Broken Web   83
Living the Good News   90
We are Free and Kept Alive by Hope: Thoughts on Resurrection   94

Ten Tips for Practical Praying   99

Appendix 1 The Iona Community   103

Appendix 2 Trident Ploughshares   106

Appendix 3 Some Useful Addresses and Websites   108

Bibliography   110

Preface

I am immensely grateful to the Swarthmore Lecture Committee for giving me the challenge of writing about the spiritual basis of activism and for the support it has given me in my ponderings and searchings. Thanks are especially due to my two support people, Helen Carmichael and Harvey Gillman for answering my calls for help, to Peter Daniels for editing at long distance, and to the prayerful upholding of Dunblane Meeting.

Over the years of my active engagement with movements for peace and social change I have written many articles about the practical aspects of activism, but it has been a real privilege to be asked to reflect deeply on the roots and motives for action, and just what I mean by prayer in my own life.

In exploring the nature of prayer, I have been led down many thrilling pathways in pursuit of the very basis of my faith. In so doing I have found myself questioning long-held tenets of belief, taking nothing for granted, and leaving no stone unturned in my pursuit of truth. But I have also learned to redefine those things that really are fundamental to me, discovering a sure and rock-solid foundation.

The title No Extraordinary Power comes from a poem by the American writer Adrienne Rich which has long been a personal favourite (see page 79). The paradox of the title is the basic theme throughout this book. Do we have access through prayer and action to some kind of "extra-ordinary" power beyond ourselves, or is our power for action well within the experience of everyone, with only our deeper spiritual nature to make it "extra-ordinary"? I leave it with the reader to decide.

Introduction

In your imagination I invite you to join me at meeting for worship at the North Gate of Faslane Naval Base, home to Britain's four Trident nuclear submarines. It is a bright, cold day with the distant hills dusted lightly with snow. Against this bright beauty, etched on the skyline, is the huge bulk of the shiplift shed where one of the subs is lurking, an unseen sinister presence. Cranes point accusing fingers to the sky. All the time a constant stream of traffic – delivery vans, busloads of workers, lorries laden with machinery, smart cars – lines up to enter the high electronically operated gates. Police armed with sub-machine guns check each driver's identity as the huge gates slide open. The wakeful eyes of the infra-red cameras top the fence, guarded by coil upon coil of high-tensile razor wire, glistening as the barbs catch the sunlight. Menace amidst beauty.

On the roundabout opposite the entrance a small band of ten or twelve folks is sitting quietly in a circle holding Quaker meeting for worship. This is organised on a regular basis by West Scotland Monthly Meeting. The traffic thunders ceaselessly around the little group, but the circle seems to contain a deep well of profound stillness. Across the road a policeman hefts his machine gun nervously and shifts from foot to foot as if slightly embarrassed. Several passing cars sound their horns in support, one or two drivers roll down their windows and shout abuse. Still the silence remains and the peace banners flap lazily in the wind. After an hour, hands are shaken, camp chairs folded up, a farewell wave to the police, and the group quietly disperses. Another small act of witness is over.

So what was going on? Prayer undoubtedly. Earnest sincere prayer, so deep as to be almost tangible. And witness, too. This was prayer over against a background of unimaginable violence. Prayer as protest, speaking truth to power in its own way, deliberately placing itself in the full public gaze in opposition to military might.

What were they expecting? Why didn't the gates of the Base collapse, the fence crumble like the walls of Jericho, the police throw down their weapons, and the whole military structure unravel before the overwhelming might of effective prayer? Or was something more subtle expected? Something more personal, maybe a small shift in attitude, a small challenge to someone's conscience. Or was the answer to prayer perhaps to be found in the comfort, strength and encouragement given to the worshippers, simply an opportunity to feel each other's support and companionship?

Certainly this was prayer, whether or not it was answered. But what of the next day, when a few hundred people gathered at the same gates and blockaded the Base for seven hours by sitting in the road, preventing the traffic from entering or leaving? Here also was passion, deep commitment, a sincerity of purpose to oppose the immorality of nuclear weapons. Was that too a form of prayer? And, if so, was it more effective in that it actually physically stopped the work of destruction, even for a short time?

This book is an exploration of some of those questions; of the links between prayer and activism – why we pray, how we go about it; to whom we think we are praying, and how prayer is effective. It is even about whether we pray at all, or if prayer is an outworn concept which may have long outlived its relevance in modern society.

Part One *Growing into Prayer*

Early Years

Throughout my life I've been conscious of a paradox. I've never
been very good at prayer, yet my whole background and upbringing
have emphasised its importance in spiritual development, and
I am most certainly well aware of the difference it does make in
my everyday life. If it is so vital, and so beneficial, why then is it so
difficult and why do I make such a chore of it?

I was brought up in the Church of Scotland in the Presbyterian
tradition. If one were to attempt to typify the different denomin-
ational characteristics, then the Church of Scotland would be
identified by its emphasis on "the Word of God" rather than on
a prescribed liturgy. When the minister comes into church he is
always preceded by the Bible, the preaching of the sermon is an
essential central part of the service, and prayers, if not nowadays
extempore, are certainly formulated by the minister. Indeed there
are still some traditions of the Presbyterian Church, especially in
the highlands and islands of Scotland, where prayers prepared
in advance would be frowned upon as lacking sincerity. In some
ways it is very close to Friends' experience of being moved by
the Spirit and not coming to meeting with a set text in mind.

I was fortunate in my church in Glasgow. It was a university
church with a very radical minister, who preached pacifism and
an active social Gospel in vivid and beautifully crafted sermons.
Indeed I owe a great debt of gratitude to Stuart McWilliam for
shaping and inspiring my spiritual development. However,
I became increasingly aware of the centrality of the minister and
the somewhat arbitrary accident that allows some congregations an
excellent minister and others a mediocre one, along with the undue
influence that such unequal distribution of talent can have on the
worshippers. Presbyterian doctrine emphasises the "priesthood of
all believers" yet the words of the sermon and the prayers were not
mine, they were the minister's, and much as I might be in accord
with the sentiments expressed, there was no place in the service for
debate, questioning or disagreement. One way of dealing with this

was to fill up the liturgical framework of praise, repentance and intercession with one's own thoughts and prayers, but this seemed to contain an inherent dishonesty. So, I listened, often appreciating the words and the sheer beauty of expression, often challenged and inspired, but liturgical prayer, for all its freedom, remained for me somewhat distant and formal.

So what of personal prayer? In this respect I was strongly influenced by the evangelical Christian tradition. Throughout my schooldays I attended Scripture Union, and I later became an enthusiastic member of a house church. Here was a much more personal approach – a direct, almost conversational relationship with God, as one to whom one could talk like a close friend. "Take it to the Lord in prayer" was the expected norm; regular daily prayer was encouraged and nothing seemed too trivial or unimportant for Jesus' attention. I must confess that in some of these prayer circles I did wonder whether Jesus was really bothered about fixing the washing machine, or whether sleeping in was a mortal sin, but there was no doubting the immediacy, sincerity and day-by-day practicality of such prayer. Our house church was a wonderfully supportive faith community undergirded by a strong and vibrant prayer life that was almost palpable.

So why then was I so bad at prayer? Every now and then I would be re-convinced of my sins of omission and start afresh, setting aside regular time for prayer and Bible study. I would try new ways of doing it; I would even write down promises to myself, but it never lasted very long; the pressures of a busy life would get in the way, and I would be left with an uneasy feeling of guilt and inadequacy.

Perhaps at the root of my problem was a basic questioning of the whole concept of prayer, and a real dichotomy between what I was supposed to believe about prayer and my actual experience in real life. Too often prayer seemed to be equated with success, and in some elements of the evangelical tradition this even meant material success in business affairs.

This understanding of prayer seems to me to marginalise weakness and failure. Are poor health, poverty, lack of business acumen all the consequence of lack of faith or sin? Surely this is the very antithesis of Jesus' life and teaching. And what about unanswered prayer? My mother died when I was nineteen. My father and I certainly prayed and prayed fervently, but for what? That she should be healed from her cancer? Somehow I knew in my innermost being that this would not happen. So was I praying for myself, for strength? And always that lingering feeling that the fault lay with my own lack of faith.

Perhaps I was praying the wrong prayer.

> I asked for strength that I might achieve;
> He made me weak that I might obey.
> I asked for health that I might do greater things;
> I was given grace that I might do better things.
> I asked for riches that I might be happy;
> I was given poverty that I might be wise.
> I asked for power that I might receive the praise of men;
> I was given weakness that I might feel the need of God.
> I asked for all things that I might enjoy life;
> I was given life that I might enjoy all things.
> I received nothing that I asked for, all that I hoped for.
> My prayer was answered.
>
> Poem from *Nurses' Christian Fellowship of
> Scotland Newsletter*, 1966 (in Steven 1988)

This seemed to be an intellectual cop-out. There are so many books that do tell of apparently miraculous instances of healing in response to prayer. So why does it work for some and not others? And yet with all these questions, I was unable to "let go" of prayer.

A Praying Community

In 1981 I became a member of the Iona Community. The Iona Community is a radical ecumenical Christian community with a membership of around 250 (see Appendix 1). It was founded in 1938 by George MacLeod, a Church of Scotland minister who perceived that the church of the time was failing to address the social needs of post-Depression Scotland. Fired by his inspiration, a group of trainee ministers and craftsmen worked together over the next 30 years to rebuild the monastic buildings of the ancient Abbey on Iona, off the west coast of Scotland, as a sign of work and worship coming together. Had that been the sum total of their endeavour we might have boosted the tourist industry, but that was never George MacLeod's vision. This ending to one of his prayers gives some insight into what he intended.

> Take us outside, O Christ, outside holiness,
> out to where soldiers curse and nations clash
> at the crossroads of the world.
> So shall this building continue to be justified.
>
> (Iona 2001)

His was a vision of a group of dedicated, committed Christians attempting to live out the Gospel in very practical working towards social change.

The Community has a five-fold Rule for members. We are a scattered community, living and working in all areas of Britain and beyond. Hence meeting together in small "family groups" is an essential component in our accounting to each other. We agree to account for the use of our time and our money, to meet together regularly, to work for justice and peace, and – of particular relevance here – regularly to pray and study the Bible. As can be imagined, when I joined in 1981 I found the justice and peace commitment the easiest part, and prayer the hardest.

The organisation of the prayer discipline is quite formal. There is a book of members, divided up into areas and organised over a period of a month, so that each day certain members are being prayed for. We are also asked to pray for specific concerns of the Community on certain days, and there is a prayer cycle for different countries around the world. As far as the study is concerned, members can choose their own sources of spiritual guidance. Each member accounts in writing once a year on progress in keeping the Rule.

In public worship held every day in the Abbey on Iona there is a regular morning office. Many members start their day with this. There is a kind of profound calm in the daily routine of a similar pattern of liturgy. Far from finding it boring or repetitious, I have often found new light or deeper meaning emerging from the repetition of familiar words, and every time I return to Iona or meet with other Community members in worship, it is rather like coming home to old familiar ways. There is a certain strength too in the knowledge that all the members are praying together in the same way. And of course constant repetition means that it is learned by heart and can be said at any time in any place. Similar in many ways to the loving familiarity with which Anglicans approach the words of the Book of Common Prayer, or Muslims know the Qu'ran. There is a common bond and instant recognition.

So why do I find this form of prayer more acceptable? At first, as a newcomer to the Community, I couldn't see the point of praying for a whole list of people I had never met, but over the years, as I came to know and love these people, just the simple act of naming them once a month brings their familiar faces to mind, and often jogs the memory into writing that overdue letter, phoning to ask after someone's health, repairing a broken trust. This kind of prayer discipline is rather like the glue that binds us together as a Community.

But is it sufficient? Words can become dogma, repetition can become convention, questioning and exploring can be stifled and challenge avoided. It can be a good starting point, but I feel that prayer must go beyond this into uncharted waters.

The Iona Community's prayer life also includes a Prayer Circle for Healing, and every Tuesday a service of prayers for healing and the laying on of hands is held in the Abbey on Iona. While for many this offers huge solace and comfort, for me it is the most difficult service of the week. During the first part of the service names of people for whom prayers have been requested are read out – and there are many, many names. We are not told what they are suffering from, as the Iona Community resists defining people in terms of what seems to be wrong with them, but as they have all been requested someone present at that service will know.

In the second part of the service those who wish to participate in the laying on of hands go forward and kneel, and all take part, both as healers and healed, linked together in a chain of loving touch. The words said over each person are: "Spirit of the Living God, present with us now, enter you, body, mind and spirit, and heal you of all that harms you." The Iona Community stresses that such prayers are not necessarily for physical healing, but for "whatever harms you", and it also makes it very clear that there are no special "healers" as such, but that God's spirit of healing love is channelled through the prayers and love of one's companions. In this context the physical experience of the loving touch of fellow worshippers is tangible and powerfully moving.

But what about that list of names? Who needs to know? Are we not already in the hands of God, who numbers the hairs on our heads and is closer than breathing? Surely God doesn't need a shopping list. Ourselves? This would make more sense if we knew what practical things we could do to help. The people being prayed for or those who requested the prayers? What are they expecting? And what about all the countless other people not on the list? Are they any less deserving of our prayers?

Experiments with Prayer

All my life I have acknowledged the importance of prayer, and
I have been fascinated and often moved and inspired by different
methods of praying. Being a somewhat undisciplined late riser,
I have always found setting aside a time every day almost impossible.
However, I have made frequent attempts. In my early days I tried
following a Scripture Union daily lectionary, but all too often
I lapsed, and somehow many of the prayers seemed somewhat
trite and rather glib.

The Iona Community commitment to Bible study is not
confined to the set canon of scripture, but can be the study of a
commentary or any inspirational book. This approach I have always
found particularly helpful. Professor Willie Barclay's commentaries
were popular reading in my early years; an *Anthology of Hope*,
compiled by my father in the years following my mother's death,
has been a constant source of inspiration; *Gifts and Discoveries* I found
wonderfully enriching and I am looking forward to *Hearts and
Minds Prepared*. Ched Myers' *Binding the Strong Man* and Walter
Wink's books on *The Powers* I found deeply challenging (although
somewhat heavy theological going for an early morning read!).

Often I struggle with these texts, finding some too hard to
understand, others too facile, and sometimes I profoundly disagree:
but as prayer is dialogue, then argument and questioning are
essential parts of that spiritual engagement.

The Bible speaks of Jacob wrestling with an angel in actual
physical terms, giving a kind of biblical image of sumo wrestling.
I prefer to think of it as a metaphor for the kind of mental wrestling
that takes place as one challenges the whole basis of one's faith,
leaving nothing unquestioned, nothing too sacred for critical
scrutiny and analysis. Recently I have been reading *Jesus Against
Christianity* by Jack Nelson-Pallmeyer and have found it one of
the most profoundly disturbing and exciting books that I have
encountered for a long time. In it he points out that the God
portrayed in the Hebrew Bible, and often in the Christian Bible,

is pathologically violent and vindictive, and that the message of
Jesus has been grossly distorted and overlaid to the point where it
is almost lost. Pallmeyer highlights how such fundamental beliefs
subconsciously and even overtly influence our present political and
social world order, giving justification for militarism, xenophobia
and religious and cultural exclusivity. Writings such as this have
challenged the way I worship, my whole cultural belief framework
and ultimately the way I respond in action. They are deeply
disturbing, making a kind of spiritual battleground of my soul,
but at the same time the whole exercise is profoundly exciting,
and uncovers new nuggets of faith to be treasured.

Many people have found Ignatian spiritual exercises to be
a helpful approach to prayer. My own first encounter with Ignatian
spirituality was during a week on Iona led by Gerry Hughes.
The theme of the week was "The Spiritual basis of Peacemaking",
and on the first day we all turned up notebooks at the ready and
pens poised. Gerry told us to put them away – we were going to
spend the week praying. I must confess that some of us activists
felt a little niggle of disappointment. It turned out to be a brilliant
week.

Our first exercise was to read a selected passage from the Bible
very carefully. We then meditated in silence on the passage, freeing
our minds of extraneous thoughts and letting a word or phrase
come to the surface. It was a profound experience, freeing the
imagination and bringing up totally unexpected insights.

The passage we were studying was the story of Jesus appearing
to his disciples in the upper room after the crucifixion. In my
imagination I was vividly present in that room with the disciples,
downcast, bewildered, all our hopes and dreams in ruins, terrified
that we might be hunted down by the Roman authorities. Suddenly
our meditations were interrupted by a knock at the door, and a
workman stuck his head into the room, saw that we were busy,
apologised and withdrew. That intrusion of reality into my
imagination of the scene made me keenly aware of real, actual,

physical fear, so that Jesus' subsequent words, "Don't be afraid", suddenly became acutely relevant.

On another day, we reflected on a very familiar Gospel story, and then through guided meditation imagined ourselves into the scene as one of the characters. By asking about smells, tastes, sounds, scenery, feelings, we were able to engage in an almost physical way with stories whose meanings had long since become dulled by sheer familiarity. They became real in a very personal way, and I have found meaning to emerge from the passage which has had a profound influence on my life.

The passage we were studying was the occasion when the rich young man came to Jesus wanting to become a follower and was advised to give away all he had and follow. As I imagined myself into the scene I was in my own home, which at that time was a rented house among some rather snobbish suburban neighbours. I pictured Jesus and his disciples as young men and women travelling around in an old clapped-out van. They were rushing around in all the hubbub of leaving on a journey, collecting sandwiches, rolling up sleeping bags, cramming luggage into the back of the van. Meanwhile a fairly dapper neighbour from up the road had arrived and was seated on our wall engaged in a deep conversation with Jesus while all the confusion eddied around them. Then in a flurry of activity they were off, leaving the young man standing in our front garden, bereft and challenged beyond his power to respond. It was up to us to help him pick up the pieces and sort out his future. I, surrounded by the Iona Community's emphasis on the Gospel for the poor, was suddenly challenged by a Gospel to the rich.

This is a method far removed from biblical scholarship and debate, although good background information and scholarship can often shed light on the text and underpin the passage. Its very subjectivity can often be an inspiration to action, drawing out new, very personal, meaning.

I may add that on the last day of that week Gerry Hughes suggested that we bring pens and paper to the last session, and the ideas for practical peace action were almost bouncing off the page.

Are prayer and inspiration interchangeable words and experiences? If so, then I have frequently been challenged by the imaginative use of biblical role-play, bibliodrama as it is sometimes called. In this method, after studying a particular biblical passage, one chooses a role within it, imagines oneself fully into the role, often with the help of some direct questions, and then the scene is played out. This has led to some of the deepest and most challenging spiritual experiences of my life, and I have seen it have a profound effect on others too, as one moves from a purely intellectual understanding of a familiar passage into the area of personal experience and imagination. I will touch on this further, but for the moment I would want to include bibliodrama as a powerful form of prayer.

Of course prayer need not be anything so formal. I am an enthusiastic hill walker and some of my very deepest spiritual moments have come when I have been walking in the mountains. The feel of warm rough rock under my fingers, the blue shadows in the ice at the edge of a snow ridge, the rough buffeting of a sea breeze, the sparkle of sun on sea and silver-streaked ocean, the scent of heather and bog myrtle – all bring me a closer awareness of the Creator. Working through a painting to satisfaction, or standing engrossed before a van Gogh; experiencing the profound calm of the slow movement of Beethoven's fourth piano concerto; being wrung out emotionally in the catharsis of a deep drama – all of these I believe are forms of prayer – of coming into contact with a dimension beyond our own at a profound level.

I also do a lot of hill walking on my own, and it is then that I have my dialogues with God, attempting to thrash out theological questions, having arguments, expressing puzzlement, distress or anger. Such discussions feel close and intimate and often help me towards decisions or clearness for the way forward. For me, this almost constant awareness of the presence of God means that conversation is always possible, and is more precious to me than the formal necessities of time and place.

New Encounters

In 1972 I left my teaching job in Glasgow to work with the Gordon Barclay Vietnam Fund. This was a Quaker project working in orphanages in Saigon. Our international team worked with a team of Vietnamese teachers to bring pre-school playgroups to three Catholic and three Buddhist orphanages, and we also worked with a toy factory run by Buddhist monks. This experience was to change my life, but here I want to note my first encounter with Buddhism and also with Friends.

I attended Buddhist classes for eighteen months, and can still bring vividly to mind the meditation garden just down the road from us in Saigon. Saigon at war was a busy cacophony of noise. The Buddhist temple was on the roof of Vanh Han, the Buddhist university. It was situated in the middle of a roof garden, constructed in such a way that the walls sloped outwards and up, to create an illusion of a grassy lawn stretching up to the blue sky, shutting out all the noise and clamour. There were blossom trees and ponds with lotus flowers, and in the midst, a very small temple, with tiny bells all round the roof, which tinkled minutely in the breeze, making one of those tiny sounds that actually enhances silence. It was a wonderful oasis of calm in the midst of all the clamour and cacophony of war, and it was easy to become lost in meditation very quickly, focussing on the gentle rise and fall of one's own breath, shutting out all distractions and thoughts of self. Here indeed I encountered a Being who was closer than breathing.

To a westernised activist intent on "doing" rather than "being" it could seem that this form of prayer, wonderfully calming as it might be, was self-indulgent escapism, particularly as some of the monks and nuns who were deeply engaged in social change work, might suddenly take themselves off into the forest to meditate for unspecified periods of time – anything from three days to three years. And yet these same monks and nuns were some of the most politically active people I have ever met, engaging in dangerous anti-war activity. Indeed shortly before our time in Vietnam, a young Buddhist schoolteacher, Nhat Chi Mai, had immolated herself as a protest against the war. She wrote:

> I join my hands and kneel down;
> I accept this utmost pain in my body
> In the hopes that the words of my heart be heard.

(Chagnon & Luce 1974)

This was not simply an extreme form of protest; this action of ultimate self-sacrifice was considered to be the highest possible form of prayer.

Here too in Saigon I experienced Quaker worship for the first time – in many ways similar to Buddhist meditation in the quiet centring down, finding the depths of stillness, and the recognition of a spiritual reality at the very core of being.

Our meeting for worship took place in an upstairs room of our house in Saigon. The walls were simply bamboo shutters that rolled up, allowing a cooling breeze to blow through the room, letting us hear the gentle rustle of the palm leaves in the breeze. However, it was rarely quiet or peaceful, and the constant clatter of helicopters overhead, the strident horns of army trucks, and the occasional burst of gunfire were a constant reminder of a bitter war being waged around us, bringing to mind all the distressing sights and experiences of our week's work. Somehow, in a most remarkable way this reminder of a perilous world deepened our worship together.

In many ways, in the profundity of the silence I found similarities between Quaker worship and Buddhist meditation. However, in contrast to the very direct personal experience of Buddhism, I have found meeting for worship to be a corporate activity. I am always conscious of the presence of the others in the room and of the power of the Spirit present in a gathered meeting, and sometimes another has ministered the very thoughts that were in my own heart. Often arising from the strength of the gathered meeting have come difficult decisions, exciting challenges and calls to prophetic action.

One of the greatest challenges to my whole upbringing and cultural environment arose out of my encounters with the American Friends. American Friends Service Committee had been working in Vietnam for many years in a rehabilitation centre in Quang Ngai near the demilitarised zone, where they made and fitted prostheses for people who had lost limbs in the war. These Friends were highly skilled, motivated people working in a situation of considerable danger and they had developed a highly political, well-informed stance against the war. Always sailing "close to the wind" with the authorities, they taught me an enormous amount about committed faith in action.

It was for this strong synthesis of deep spiritual awareness and practical action in the world that I, and so many others over the centuries, have become attracted to the Society of Friends.

Another valuable Quaker tradition from Fox onwards that I have found particularly helpful as an aid to prayer, is that of writing a journal. Here at last I found a truly useful method of prayer that spoke directly to my condition, combining as it does the discipline of daily reflection, quiet time and exploration of my own leadings. I found it an indispensable source of strength when my partner, Ellen Moxley, was in prison over a period of four and a half months for an act of witness as part of Trident Ploughshares, and I felt utterly bereft. I found that taking half an hour in the early morning, sitting quietly with a passage from *Quaker Faith and Practice*, and then writing down my personal thoughts and reflections, gave me courage, quietness and purpose for the whole day. By contrast, days when I omitted this time of quiet became confused and disorganised. It is perhaps ironic that so often it takes a crisis to make us resort to the sheer pleasure of prayer and reflection.

Sometimes prayer can be expressed in very practical, almost ritualistic actions. The lighting of a candle, the throwing of a pebble, the writing of a message on a piece of paper either to destroy or treasure, making oneself a promise on a postcard: all these I believe are aids to prayer. I personally found a very helpful way of dealing with despair using one of these practical forms of prayer. It was soon after the disaster at Chernobyl, and I found myself in the depths of despair, unable even to plant my garden, so convinced was I of the futility of it all. Realising that I was facing a spiritual crisis, I copied out a form of creed used in Iona Abbey. It states, "We believe in God, who is love and who has given the earth to all people."

I took a piece of paper and very deliberately wrote the opposite: "I believe in a God who is malevolent and who has given the earth to the rich and the Ministry of Defence." Then suddenly I could go no further, and took a big red felt-pen and wrote NO across the page. It was a small gesture of defiance, but it rekindled a tiny flame of hope and resistance.

This almost forlorn resistance was acted out for me in May 1985 when I was part of a CND protest at the gates of RNAD Coulport, a huge arms depot, where the nuclear missiles for Trident are stored in bunkers underground. A small group of us were chained together across the gates, kneeling in prayer at the feet of a double cordon of police. When the Chief of Police came out to caution and then arrest us, he said rather dismissively, "Well, now that you've done your sacrificial lamb bit, perhaps you'd like to run along home." Fortunately someone near me managed to forestall my instinct to bite the police chief's ankle, by saying quite gently, "This may not matter to you, but it's very important to us." Useless, pathetic? Or a highly symbolic way of praying?

Some Awkward Questions

So far we have been dealing purely with the mechanics, the how and the what of prayer, but not the why. I am conscious that huge assumptions are made, and that the deep underlying questions have not yet been addressed. I will shortly be addressing some of the ways in which I have used prayer or found it helpful in my life as an activist and campaigner, and I will look at the way in which the spiritual dimension of the prayer life and the acting out in the world inform and inspire each other. But I do not wish to escape or avoid some fundamental questions.

Whom are we praying to when we pray? Is God immanent or transcendent? If we are praying to a God who is found in our innermost being, then is our prayer purely subjective? Prayer is often not answered. Does this mean that we are praying for the wrong things, or that we lack the necessary faith, or that God is not omnipotent? Do words and forms matter in prayer, are they helpful or a barrier? What is actually happening when we pray? Are we simply meeting our own psychological needs, or even inadequacies, or is there something/someone beyond? Does prayer make any difference? Is prayer only answered by our own actions, in which case do we need to pray at all? Do numbers matter? If a large number of people are praying for a specific situation, is that more efficacious than one heartfelt prayer, or is it creating a kind of numinous climate of change?

This section has described some of the influences that have shaped my prayer life and my commitment to action. In Part Two I will consider some of the different aspects of what prayer might be, and then in Part Three I will make an attempt to address some of the awkward questions and explain my own understanding of prayer.

Part Two *Aspects of Prayer*

The Everlasting Arms: Prayer as Upholding

Perhaps the form of prayer that most of us are most comfortable
and familiar with is that of supporting or upholding prayer. How
often do people who might not otherwise seem to have religious or
spiritual affiliations say "Pray for me", usually in all sincerity? Is this
simply a kind of rabbit's foot talisman, a celestial insurance policy,
or is there some deep-seated human need urging us towards prayer?
Undoubtedly there is a strong human need to uphold each other
and be upheld.

In the Iona Community's daily morning liturgy, we name
Community members individually in a prayer rotation on a certain
day of the month, and we end each naming with the words, "May
they not fail you", and respond, "Nor we fail them". Quite apart
from the warm feeling of support from the entire Community
on "your own" day, there is also a strong element of mutual
accountability and responsibility towards each other, that is a
fundamental part of the Community's five-fold Rule. It is a mutual
support network with a purpose and a challenge.

One of the strongest personal experiences I have had of being
upheld by the prayers of others was during my first time in prison
in 1985. I had been arrested for planting potatoes inside the nuclear
submarine base at Faslane on the Clyde, as a sign of growing food
for the hungry rather than threatening planetary destruction. On
refusing to pay my fine, I was given a minimum five-day sentence.
I had expected prison to be a rich experience, providing me with the
time for spiritual exploration. As a person following my conscience,
I was looking forward to a deeply rewarding time.

Nothing could have been further from the truth. I found prison
difficult, unsettling, far too distressing to allow me the leisure to
focus my mind. I was in a spiritual desert. As I sat there on my bed
castigating myself for being such a moral failure, I looked across
to the shelf opposite, filled with a magnificent array of cards and
goodwill messages. It was like sinking back into a soft downie,
being wrapped and enfolded in the love of God and my friends.

I didn't need to pray – I was being warmly and strongly upheld by the prayers of all my friends.

It is worth noting in passing, however, that I would never have known about all this love surrounding me, if my friends had not taken the trouble to send me tangible tokens in the form of written messages and cards. Is this perhaps a clue to how prayer works: that our care and concern is expressed through very practical expressions of support?

The simple words "I'll pray for you" can be hugely encouraging. Some years ago I organised a meeting of military generals, top civil servants and defence experts, coming together with assorted peace campaigners and church leaders for a week on Iona. At the start of the week I was understandably nervous, and a guest at the Abbey who was not a participant in the conference came up to me and said, "Would you like me to pray for you all during the conference?" I accepted her offer, rather with the attitude of "Oh well, if she would like to do that it can't do any harm." From time to time throughout the week we would meet in passing and she would simply give me a little nod of acknowledgement. Gradually I realised that the knowledge of her prayerful support was becoming more and more significant. By the end of a truly amazing week, I realised just how important her prayers had been. Not just that I personally felt calmed and supported by her thoughts; it was also a tapping into some kind of intangible energy that could be felt at our meetings. I think we were all surprised, and one of the military men summed it up with his parting words as he stepped onto the ferry: "Only the hand of God could have dumped me into the midst of a bunch of raving peace women!" Then he looked me directly in the eye and said, "And I mean it."

This highlights a crucially important form of activism, that of the prayerful supporter. For some years our nonviolent action group was supported by a nun in an enclosed Carmelite order. Most of us never met her, but she wanted to know whenever we were doing an action or had an important decision to make, so that she could uphold us in prayer. I believe it strengthened our group in unseen ways, and I also believe strongly that her prayers were as valid a form of activism as our demonstrations and protests, but that one without the complementary activity of the other has an inherent weakness and lack of balance.

Friends speak of holding someone in the Light and I have always found this a particularly helpful way of expressing it. The idea of going beyond words to a different level of being, to enfold another in the Light and Love beyond our physical experience, is a very attractive image.

A powerful example of "holding someone in the Light" occurred during the trial of the Trident Three at Greenock Sheriff Court. Ellen Moxley, Ulla Roder and Angie Zelter were on trial for dismantling part of the acoustic testing facility for the Trident nuclear submarines by throwing the computers into the Loch. The three maintained that their actions were to uphold international law, basing their defence on the ruling of the International Court of Justice in the Hague in July 1996 that nuclear weapons are in contravention of international humanitarian law. Only a few days into the trial Sheriff Margaret Gimblett was faced with a crucial decision whether or not to allow this defence under international law or to treat it as a straightforward case of criminal damage. Everything hinged on her decision. She adjourned the court while she considered the case. Immediately a small group gathered on the pavement outside the court and stood in silence holding Margaret Gimblett in the Light. In many ways similar to upholding the Clerk at Yearly Meeting, this was one of the most powerful experiences of focused prayer that I have ever had. An hour later the Court reconvened, and her decision to allow a defence under international law became legal and campaigning history, as the trial moved on to the acquittal of the Trident Three four and a half weeks later. Sheriff Margaret Gimblett's profoundly moving summing up reflects the moral courage of the decision she took, influenced, I am certain, by the power of prayer.

I have the invidious task of deciding on international law as it relates to nuclear weapons. I am only a very junior sheriff without the wisdom or experience of those above me. I have a knowledge of the repercussions which could be far-reaching. As a sheriff I took an oath to act without fear or favour in interpreting the law…I have to conclude that the three accused, in company with many others, were justified in thinking that Great Britain's use and deployment of Trident…could be construed as a threat…and as such is an infringement of international and customary law. I have heard nothing which would make it seem to me that the accused acted with criminal intent. Therefore I will instruct the jury that they should acquit the three accused. (Gimblett 1999)

Finding a Way: Prayer as Guidance and Discernment

All of us face moments of decision and choice in our lives, sometimes all too obviously as we agonise and worry over the way ahead, sometimes choices that are only seen in retrospect, when a parting of ways has been seen in context. We come to such decisions in a variety of ways: seeking advice from friends, holding a meeting for clearness, going into quiet retreat, weighing up options on sheets of paper; or sometimes momentous decisions can almost be made by seeming accident or coincidence. But are such choices really random, or the result of a series of processes? Is there truly a "right way", and is it possible to receive divine guidance or find ways beyond ourselves of following leadings? George MacLeod, the founder of the Iona Community, is often quoted as saying, "If you think that's a coincidence, may you lead a dull life!"

There have been several times in my own life when I have been made aware of difficult or challenging decisions to be made, and I have used a variety of ways of seeking guidance.

Perhaps here it is necessary to go a step backwards and consider
what it is that precipitates the need to make decisions at all. What is
it that occasionally pitches us out of the comfortable place we are
in, to face a challenge, or seek adventure, or follow new untrodden
paths? Very often there is a distinct shift away from carefully
considered, rational decisions – a weighing up of the pros and cons
– into an uncharted area of the subconscious or realm of feeling
and emotion. Is this perhaps the reason why so many of the biblical
references to times of choice are expressed in terms of dreams and
visions? In other words, is there an acknowledgement that some of
our choices belong to a realm of the spiritual that defies description,
and that rationality has to take second place?

Personally, I have never experienced guidance or inspiration
directly from dreams, in spite of coming from a distant heritage in
which "the second sight" was a recognised cultural and spiritual
phenomenon. In fact I remain distinctly sceptical and ambivalent
about any kind of prediction of the future that might suggest a
predestined course mapped out by an all-knowing God. However,
just because such experiences are not within my own experience is
not to deny that some people, perhaps more acutely in touch with
their subconscious, do receive guidance and insight from visions
and dreams, and indeed take the trouble to pay attention to their
dreams. At a more superficial level, I have certainly found the old
advice to "sleep on it" a helpful way of resolving problems. I have
often gone to bed with a problem exercising my mind and wakened
in the morning to greater clarity. Perhaps this has something to do
with letting go and sinking into a deeper subconscious level where
the rational mind is stilled and the creative imagination takes over.

In his book *God of Surprises*, Gerry Hughes, a Jesuit priest,
describes the spiritual exercises of St Ignatius. Much of this book
I have found of great value in my experiments with prayer. From the
very start there is a helpful emphasis on the ease and comfort of
prayer, not as a hard discipline laid upon us in which we constantly
fall short, but rather as a practice as natural as breathing or brushing

our teeth. He says, "There are as many ways of praying as there are human beings. Everyone has the ability to pray and each must find their own way." This emphasis on the personal nature of prayer leads to a total freedom from the constraints and expectations of the institutional church. In a passage which rings true in the experience of Friends, he says, "If the mystical element is not emphasised in the Church, and if we do not meet God within our own unique inner selves, our religion can degenerate into an idolatry of the institution, or the worship of an ideology, a system of ideas." (Hughes 1987, pp. 40–41 and 93)

I include the Ignatian method of praying because I have found it particularly helpful when trying to make decisions. There is a sense in which the "rightness" of our actions is known by the feelings of happiness, joy, comfort that we experience from being in a right relationship with God. "If the core of our being is directed to God, then our creative moods, feelings, actions and decisions will bring peace, joy and tranquillity, while the destructive elements within us will bring agitation, sadness, inner turmoil."

This is not a glib, facile "feel-good" syndrome, nor is it a kind of floating through life as a Pollyanna with a Zen smile. These feelings of deep inner awareness can come at times of deep pain and sorrow. Indeed the very fact of our sorrow is in itself proof of the rightness at the core of one's being. There are situations in our world where we would be pathologically disturbed not to feel sorrow.

Gerry Hughes writes of times of "consolation" or "desolation", of being in tune or out of tune. Such creative moods, says Hughes, are known by their effect, in an increase of faith and hope and, of course, resulting in action. This is not a spirituality divorced from the real world. We are encouraged to develop our awareness of these inner moods almost by letting them creep up and surprise us.

This is a deeply intuitive way of seeking discernment and one that I personally have found very helpful over the years, as I have been so often blessed with a deep sense of happiness resulting from the privilege of being enabled to work at the issues that most concern me.

Leaving the Comfort Zone: Prayer as Challenge

As mentioned above, I spent two years working in orphanages in Saigon. This was perhaps the most significant decision of my life. Various factors contributed to what became one of the most radical shifts in my life. One was almost certainly circumstance.

My mother died when I was nineteen and since then I had been looking after my father and younger brother. When my father remarried, I was free to leave home and travel, although it took a few years for this change in my circumstances to dawn on me. Certainly at that time in my life I was a praying person, in a conventional sense, and there was a fairly persistent nagging in my mind that kept telling me that teaching in a fee-paying girls' school in Glasgow, enjoyable and fulfilling as it was, was somehow too comfortable and safe. I believed that God was calling me to do something different, new and exciting with my life. It was a kind of "discomfort zone" coupled with a strong blend of Presbyterian guilt.

Following the prompting of this annoying "still, small voice" I applied to various agencies for voluntary work overseas. Several opportunities presented themselves, but none of them seemed quite right. Until one evening in 1971, I was watching a news item about Vietnam, then at the height of the Vietnam War, and my heart was stricken by pictures of Vietnamese children in orphanages. I knew with absolute clarity that that was where I had to go. It was a purely emotional response, at a deep gut level, and also informed by a kind of altruistic "I must do something for these poor suffering children".

Looked at in retrospect these were all the wrong reasons for going. I had little or no background knowledge of Vietnam and was politically very naïve; I was a secondary school history teacher with no experience of working with babies; my decision was purely emotional, with little awareness of the consequences of my actions. Later, as our team in Saigon became more immersed in the complexities of war-torn Vietnam, we became highly critical of the work we were doing, to the point where we changed the whole direction of the project, and finally left Vietnam having established a training programme for teachers running day-care centres, enabling mothers to care for their children at home rather than being forced to leave them in orphanages.

Those experiences influenced the whole of the rest of my life. In Vietnam I learned the immense value of other cultures; I came home totally committed to working for peace, having at the same time become aware of the complexities and cynicism of international politics; and the Vietnamese people gave me the confidence to find my own place in the struggle for peace and justice in my own country. Vietnam gave my life a whole new meaning and purpose. It also gave me my adopted daughter, Marian, now in her 30s and happily settled with her husband in Scotland. So in that sense at least, my decision to go to Vietnam was the right one.

There are times when the new direction comes almost against one's will, in response perhaps to the urgings or prayers of others. After I returned from Vietnam, I found myself a small cottage in a beautiful part of the country and spent a long, hot summer being very happily unemployed. My family were concerned about my future prospects and my step-mother, a deeply committed Christian, spent a whole night praying that I might be guided into a more settled and useful future. The following morning she was crumpling up a newspaper to light the fire and saw an advertisement for a job with the Iona Community as their justice and peace worker. She immediately telephoned me and urged me to apply for the post. I confess that my initial response was one of annoyance – a feeling of a conspiracy to disrupt my life out of its comfortable laid-back niche into directions I had not chosen. However, I promised at least to apply, and thus started on the best job of my life, later becoming a member of the Iona Community, which has been for me one of the greatest sources of spiritual nourishment. How often has reluctance been the initial response of those being called to new directions?

In this respect I have always been heartened by the reluctance of
Moses in responding to God's call. Here was no valiant dashing into
action, fearless unquestioning confrontation with the power-base of
Pharaoh. In fact, according to the rather honest story in Exodus, he
makes every excuse in the book. He asks how he is to describe God
to Pharaoh; then what to do if the people won't believe him; then
rather touchingly, "I have never been eloquent; I am slow of tongue
and slow of speech"; finally the most honest answer of all, "O my
Lord, please send someone else!" I think we've all been there with
Moses at some point in our lives.

One of the hardest boundaries for me to cross was my decision
to engage in civil disobedience. For a well-behaved middle-class
woman, whose whole upbringing had tended towards being
law-abiding, respectful and conforming, it was a huge step to break
the law deliberately. Again early influences, like straws in the wind,
had a part to play. I am a historian, and some of my greatest heroes
and heroines have been people whose conscience led them to take
a stand in defiance of the power of state or church laws. People like
Martin Luther – "Here I stand, I can do no other" – John Bunyan,
George Fox and early Friends, the Scottish Covenanters, Rosa
Parks, the Suffragettes and, with more immediate relevance, the
Committee of 100, have always been an inspiration to me, and
I was well aware that almost all social and religious change have
come about through such courageous acts of defiance. When I read
about nuclear protestors sailing deliberately into the test zone in the
Pacific, I was deeply moved and reminded of a poem:

> Faith is not learned from books, but, like Peter,
> by following Jesus into "impossible" situations,
> launching out into the deeps at his command,
> walking out into the stormy waters of life,
> and finding that somehow, "it works".
> Faith is not learned sitting in the armchair,
> but on the knife-edge between faith and folly,

when life and death are at stake, and only faith in God
remains between you and disaster.

(Anon, in Steven 1988)

Another source of inspiration to me was Martin Luther King,
and I was often challenged by one of my favourite passages from his
book of sermons, *Strength to Love*:

We must make a choice. Will we continue to march to the
drumbeat of conformity and respectability, or will we,
listening to the beat of a more distant drum, move to its
echoing sounds? Will we march only to the music of time, or
will we, risking criticism and abuse, march to the soul-saving
music of eternity? (King 1984)

These were inspiring words and seemed particularly apposite
to my middle-class condition, but it was quite a different matter for
me actually to do things like that. I suppose my biggest fear was
loss of credibility. Much of my work involved speaking in churches,
meeting with military people, trying to win over the uncommitted
"middle ground". Being respectable, in other words. By going to
prison I might be putting myself beyond the pale, stepping too far
outside the expected norm, becoming an extremist. Would people
pay any serious attention to what I had to say?

Then I was really worried about how I would be received by
my fellow prisoners and prison officers. Would I be regarded as a
middle-class dilettante, merely playing at prison? After all, I did have
a choice. All I had to do was pay my fine and walk free – a privilege
available to none of my fellow inmates.

And of course there was a fear of the unknown: I was afraid of
looking stupid in court, of not knowing the rules, both written and
unwritten, "inside". And many more unnamed, deep-seated fears
both rational and completely irrational, experienced by anyone who
steps outside their usual comfort zone. I lost a lot of sleep over my
decision, and was constantly questioning my choices.

On the other hand, I was in a very privileged position with

regard to civil disobedience. I was in a job which actively encouraged me to follow my conscience; I had no elderly relatives or children dependent on me for care; my family, although perhaps somewhat surprised and bewildered by my behaviour, nevertheless was very supportive. What's more, I was training other people in nonviolent resistance; the least I could do was to follow my own teaching. I really had no excuses to prevent me.

Most important of all was the motivation. I preferred to describe my actions in a positive light as Christian obedience rather than civil disobedience. There was no doubt in my own mind about the immorality of nuclear weapons. Not only was I convinced in my own heart and soul, but I also had the authority of all the major spiritual influences in my life. The Iona Community's Justice and Peace Commitment states, "We believe that the use or threatened use of nuclear and other weapons of mass destruction is theologically and morally indefensible, and that opposition to their existence is an imperative of the Christian faith" (see Appendix 1). Strong words indeed.

Our own Peace Testimony says, "We utterly deny all outward wars and strife" and then goes on to say, "The spirit of Christ is not changeable" – in other words, we cannot say that we love our enemies only for as long as it suits our national or economic interests to do so, and then will reserve the right to use our nuclear weapons.

Finally, as long ago as 1984 the General Assembly of the Church of Scotland stated categorically: "Nuclear weapons are contrary to the will of God."

These were serious statements of faith. To one who places great value on the will of God and who attempts to live in the spirit of Christ, the imperative to take action seemed unavoidable. Nor could the seriousness of such statements be adequately reflected in marches, letters or speeches, important thought they are. It seemed to me that the urgency of the imperative demanded something more. I felt deeply that I was being called to witness, but it was a hard, hard choice.

In studying the actions of those who had been my inspiration, I came to realise that their actions sprang out of careful preparation and discernment. Rosa Parks didn't spontaneously decide to make her witness at the front of the bus; she was part of a group of civil rights activists, who had undertaken serious nonviolence training and prayer. Civil rights activists kneeling in front of the police with dogs and water cannon had emerged from intense experiences of prayer and worship.

In the 1960 edition of *Christian Faith and Practice* a passage by T. Edmund Harvey advises, "Before deciding on a course which involves disobedience to the command of the State, the good citizen will seek the best guidance he (she) can obtain" (*CFP* § 584), and the current edition of *Advices and Queries* says, "If you feel impelled by strong conviction to break the law, search your conscience deeply. Ask your meeting for the prayerful support which will give you strength as a right way becomes clear" (*QFP* § 1.02 no. 35).

I knew this to be very sound advice, but at the time of my first arrest I didn't have the confidence to take it to my meeting, mainly because I thought they would disagree and try to dissuade me. Was it arrogance, lack of trust, a realistic appraisal of the situation? I only know in retrospect that in failing to test my decision with my meeting, I deprived myself of some valuable advice and a potential source of great support. However, I am well aware that such helpful sifting of decisions might not always be available, and there are times when one simply has to rely on that uncomfortable "still, small voice".

It has been significant to me that there have been times when I felt that my law-breaking was entirely justified and a genuine act of witness, and other times when I have been much less sure of my ground. The first time I was arrested I was absolutely clear that this was the right thing for me to do and that I was following a genuine call.

The next occasion when I was arrested I also felt it to be exactly right. This was the protest already mentioned when a group of us knelt in prayer, chained together across the gates of the Trident missile store at Coulport. The action was strong, dignified and deeply spiritual, and I know that many of the arresting officers were profoundly moved by it. Again I felt that I was in the right place at the right time; on both occasions a fine was imposed and I refused to pay and went to prison for a short time.

However, the third time somehow did not have the same certainty. I was participating in the Snowball Campaign, in which an initial three people cut one strand of the fence at a military base, having written statements giving their reasons to the base commander, the press and one other person. They then waited to be arrested. Subsequently nine people did it, then 81, and so on exponentially. When I did it I was one of about 500 protestors around the country all taking action on the same day. I had no quibble with the campaign itself, which was totally nonviolent, well-organised, principled and, I believe, ultimately unstoppable. More questionable were my own motives. I had not given it careful thought or prayer in advance, simply going along as one of a crowd: of course I would do it, after all I was the one who was "always getting arrested". It was a casual, almost light-hearted engagement, and carried with it a fair degree of pride and a seeking of the limelight. By the time I came to court, I was no longer so sure that I had done the right thing, and so I quietly paid my fine.

Dogged Persistence: Prayer as Importuning God

Sometimes the whole process of seeking guidance and realising our dreams can seem to be a huge struggle and take a very long time. In 1987 Ellen and I started Peace House, a residential centre in central Scotland, where people could come for courses in nonviolence and discussions of peace and justice issues. In the course of twelve years over 10,000 people came through our doors, and many people still talk with fondness of the importance of Peace House in their lives.

Few of them are aware of the long, protracted struggle we had over a period of almost ten years to realise the vision of Peace House. In retrospect I can see that various forms of prayer played a significant part, some explicit, and some inherent, almost unrecognised as prayer.

The original dream of such a centre arose partly out of the experiences both Ellen and I had had in Vietnam, and a recognition that there was work to be done for the peace movement in Scotland. We wrote out a proposal and sent it around those friends and organisations who might be supportive. Many expressed interest, one slipped it into a filing cabinet with a note pinned to it saying, "Another of Helen's pipe dreams!", and one wise friend said, "The time is not now. Put the proposal away somewhere safe, and you will know when the time is right to bring it out again." Sometimes this can be the awkward answer to prayer – to have the patience to wait, to seem to do nothing until the time is right. It is a very frustrating answer for one as impatient as I am to be up and doing and sorting out the world.

Years passed. I had a wonderfully fulfilling job with the Iona Community; then one day, quite out of the blue, two close friends, members of the Iona Community, told us that they had some money to invest, and they wanted to use it to help us launch the idea of our peace centre. Suddenly our rather vague and idealistic notion of a peace centre was pitchforked from the back of the filing cabinet into the real world. The right moment seemed to have arrived.

There was now a need for real clarity about the exact nature of the project. We decided to ask for a meeting for clearness. This practice originated in early Friends seeking guidance from the meeting on marriage, but has since widened in its remit. "By focusing on a particular issue, a meeting for clearness enables everyone present to become 'clear' about possible options and ways forward." Most meetings for clearness follow a set pattern described in *Quaker Faith and Practice* § 12.25:

Meetings for clearness should be held in a relaxed atmosphere of trust yet a certain degree of formality is helpful. A facilitator should be chosen to assist in clarifying the question or questions to be asked. Some groups may decide that notes should be taken. It will have to be made explicit that confidentiality is to be maintained within the group. There is need for listening with undivided attention, for tact, affirmation and love for those seeking clearness.

I have used this formal process of seeking guidance on subsequent occasions and found it very helpful, but none, I think, were as crucial to our future as the one we held in 1985. We gathered a few close friends, who began by exploring with us the strengths and weaknesses we brought to the task, probing keenly and lovingly into our reasons for starting the project, and looking at the practical obstacles as well as the aids to the realisation of the dream. We were then left to work through the material on our own and reach our decisions. It was clear that we should at least proceed, but we little knew then the struggles that lay ahead.

As so often happens with transactions involving property, there were protracted complications, and we were soon launched on a roller-coaster of frustrations, excitements and disappointments, so that it seemed at times as if we were back at the beginning, and our vision as far away as ever. It was at one of these low points that a member of the family phoned me and said, "There seem to be so many obstacles in your path. You would think that if it was God's will, it would be a little more straightforward. Are you sure you're doing the right thing?" I snapped back, "Yes, of course I'm sure," and put the phone down, but of course that was precisely the question that was haunting us both. Why did it seem so difficult at every turn? Were we simply resisting a clear leading to drop the whole idea? We were in a quandary.

It was precisely at this point of need that our friend Kathy Galloway, then the warden of Iona Abbey, opened the way for what I would describe as another form of prayerful guidance. She offered us a free week staying in the Abbey to give us a clear space to grapple with our decisions. The value of taking time and a quiet space to work on important decisions cannot be over-emphasised. That week on Iona was a very special privilege.

We used the time in a variety of quite structured ways. Firstly, we knew that we were surrounded by a community of love and support which upheld us in the process but didn't interfere. Regular morning and evening worship in the Abbey and frequent long walks in the beauty of the island provided a framework. We then developed a detailed plan of action, which involved covering the floor of our room with huge sheets of flip-chart paper and felt pens. Taking absolutely nothing for granted, we went right back to basics and listed all the possible options. We developed a detailed plan of all the possible outcomes of each of these options, then made columns of the pros and cons, frequently taking time away from the papers to check our feelings and emotional response to the various paths outlined. We noted down some of the practical steps needed to develop our chosen options. It was detailed, down-to-earth planning and might seem no different from any of the strategies adopted by big business or market planning. However, set in a context of openness to the prompting of the Spirit, I would claim this to be a very valid and useful form of prayer.

By the end of the week we believed that we were still being led to go ahead with the purchase of Peace House, but we set a time limit of a year. Within a few months the sale went ahead, our first guests had arrived, and we were launched on twelve years of very hard but richly rewarding work.

Ask for What You Need: Prayer as Petition

I have never been very sure about prayers of petition. Of course there are countless examples of people who most undoubtedly admit to the power of answered prayer in their lives. Nevertheless, "Ask and you shall receive" somehow seems too glib and easy, because so many people ask and quite patently don't receive. And there can be the somewhat smug certainty of the successful and rich who maintain that their wealth and position is in some way a reward for godliness. Looked at in those terms, Jesus and his followers may have been successful in terms of the Kingdom of God, but they were remarkably unsuccessful by any worldly standards.

It is true that I have experienced a whole lifetime of answers to prayers I never knew I had made. Throughout the protracted struggle for Peace House, events seemed to happen and openings occur in most inexplicable ways. The number of properties we didn't get, realising later how inappropriate they would have been; the original loan of £10,000 making the whole project possible; the financial support we received from trust funds, Quakers, Iona Community and friends, sufficient to enable us to buy and equip a large house when we ourselves had very few resources; the offers of help both physical and material from countless friends: all of these bear witness, in retrospect, to answered prayer.

I must admit to being somewhat sceptical of the kind of request for an exact amount of money, like £349.56, being granted to the last penny, yet almost reluctantly I must admit to being in a panic about a certain lawyer's bill for a rather large amount, and that same day receiving a cheque for the exact amount in the post. I really don't believe in "that kind of thing", and yet it seems to happen. Sometimes it happens in almost comical ways. Some years ago Ellen and I were visiting peace activists in the USA and were fortunate enough to stay with Art Laffin, a member of the Jonah House Community, one of the Catholic Worker houses inspired by Dorothy Day and Daniel Berrigan. His whole life was lived in a kind of prayerful slipstream. We were being driven to an important peace meeting in Washington DC in his ancient wreck of a car when, hardly surprisingly, it quietly spluttered to a halt. With the same nonchalant confidence with which one might nowadays use a mobile phone, Art prayed. "Oh God," he said, "it is really important for your work that we reach this meeting in time, so please make the car go." It did!

The newsletter of the Catholic Worker movement is called *The Little Way* and there is a section in it which is to me the epitome of down-to-earth prayer. On the one hand it lists exactly what these houses for homeless people need: washing machines, flour for baking, a vacuum cleaner; and next to it there is a section giving thanks for answered prayer, also listing the items received over the past month. These things were not luxury items; they were essential to the needs of a poor community and it is important to stress that this kind of prayer is for what you need rather than what you want.

But abundance also seems possible. The story of how we finally arrived at our present home in the north-west of Scotland seems so unreal that I still find it almost impossible to believe. Working for the peace movement is never a very lucrative business, so over our 25 campaigning years, Ellen and I had never been able to make any savings, nor had we ever had a high enough income to obtain a mortgage. Hence we had lived in rented accommodation or tied houses all our working lives, and any thoughts of buying a house in the north-west for our retirement were distant dreams. However, we kept hopeful, and over a period of about ten years persistently visited the area looking at houses – mostly derelict! It wasn't until the summer of 2002, when I was due to retire, that events began to fall into place.

"Ask for what you need" was advice once given to us by a friend, so we walked boldly into the estate office in Lochinver and asked what was available. We were told about an old croft house near the lighthouse at Stoer Point – the very spot where twelve years earlier Ellen had said she would like to live! The house was damp, but we instantly fell in love with it. However, as houses in the area were selling at ridiculous prices as holiday homes, we put it to the back of our minds along with other unrealistic notions.

Some months later, we received a phone call to tell us that the house was still on the market and to ask if we were still interested.

Of course we were, so we took our courage in both hands and wrote to the owner explaining that we intended to live in the area, and as it was not to be a holiday house, would he consider fixing the price? A week before Christmas we received the unexpected "yes". By Christmas Eve we had checked it out with a builder, put in an offer and had it accepted.

Then the panic. We simply didn't have that kind of money. Within a couple of months to our utter amazement our friends had rallied round with offers of substantial loans and outright gifts, so that we had enough and to spare. Added to that, we had a great friend from Trident Ploughshares who was a builder, and he offered to work for us on any renovations needed.

Sitting outside on the bench in the garden, looking out to sea and fold upon fold of sparkling mountains, we are filled with deep wells of gratitude. And indeed as I look back on an interesting and exciting life as an activist, I am deeply conscious of having been cared for in a multitude of practical ways. Some might say, I suppose, that this has nothing to do with God; that it is all entirely due to the generosity and kindness of our friends, and that giving thanks to God is misplaced gratitude. To them I would say, that I believe that this is how God works: through the willingness, love and care of others.

So what is it that we are really doing with these prayers of petition? In the first place there is the question of what we are praying for. If, as Martin Luther King said, "The Universe bends towards the good", then our needs and desires have to be consonant with this general purpose of good. My happiness at the expense of another's suffering cannot be right, and if my life is indeed happy and blessed, then there is the immediate question of how I am being accountable and sharing this bounty with others around me.

Then there is also the necessity to be honest about what we need and to make personal efforts towards attaining it. Sometimes it can be very hard to swallow pride and ask for help; it is difficult to admit to weakness and imperfection; most of us like to appear to be in control. This is perhaps especially important for the energetic activist to remember. Often showing one's vulnerability and fears can open the way for others to be empowered and discover their capacity to help.

The other side of the coin is the need to use a considerable amount of personal effort and initiative in answering one's own prayers. One of my father's oft-used phrases was, "Don't keep your wishbone where your backbone ought to be!" Indeed it goes beyond this into the whole dangerous, uncharted territory of taking risks and pushing the boat out. When Peace House started, a charitable trust had given us an interest-free loan for a year. There was no obvious way of repaying this loan, and we applied to Quaker Peace and Service to take over the project. This they eventually did, by buying out the house on a fifteen-year loan. Looking back we feel sure that had we not taken the risk, gone ahead in faith and shown in the course of a year that the project was practical and worthwhile, Quaker Peace and Service would not have taken it on. There was a fine balance between taking a gamble and acting responsibly.

If prayer is often answered by the generosity or responsiveness of our friends, then where should we be directing our petitions? Sometimes God may be saying, "Go and ask the right department."

Part of the worship cycle on Iona includes a weekly service of commitment. In this, people have the opportunity to re-dedicate their lives, sometimes quietly in personal prayer, sometimes by going to the front of the congregation and kneeling, while the worship leader pronounces a saying of Jesus over each person. For me this became almost a routine, as I would re-commit myself at the end of a summer season before going back to work on the mainland. On this particular occasion, I went forward as usual, and the words for me were, "Ask and you shall receive." I went away considering these very familiar words, when suddenly it occurred to me that I was asking the wrong person. What I ardently prayed for was an end to the nuclear arms race. Why then was I asking God to deliver what was the province of the military and the politicians? Thus was born the first of the "Options for Defence" conferences to which military generals, defence experts, campaigners and church leaders were invited. These dialogues are still continuing in the regular Rhu Consultations, where there is still a really deep exchange of views and concerns.

Thus if we are seeking an answer to prayer we may be led into direct engagement with the social and political structures of power. As William Penn famously said, "True Godliness don't turn men out of the world, but enables them to live better in it, and excites their endeavours to mend it" (QFP § 23.02); or in a more contemporary context, Gordon Matthews wrote:

> We need both a deeper spirituality and a more outspoken witness. If our spirituality can reach the depths of authentic prayer, our lives will become an authentic witness for justice, peace and the integrity of creation, a witness which becomes the context for our prayer. (QFP § 23.10)

Thus prayer becomes the very mainspring of action. It was in response to inner leadings of prayer that Friends campaigned against slavery, that they dared to travel to Russia to speak with the Tsar during the Crimean war, that Amnesty International was formed, and that Mary Dyer was driven back to Massachusetts to her death. Prayer that is real can have the most unexpected results, and almost inevitably leads us into action in ways we might never have dreamed of. Prayer is essentially practical and political.

I once stayed with a group of nuns in a convent in St Louis. Part of their daily prayer involved either watching the news on television, or else reading a daily newspaper in an attitude of awareness and openness to action in response to current events.

George MacLeod used to say that it was no use praying for a woman to be cured of her TB if we were not prepared to work politically with government and local authorities to provide adequate, damp-free housing. One of the inspirational groups arising out of this essentially practical philosophy was the Gorbals Group. This was a group of young Church of Scotland ministers and committed lay people who decided that rather than praying for an end to poverty in Glasgow, they were going to live as an intentional community in the Gorbals, one of the poorest areas of the city, well-known for its violence and deprivation. Their houses were open day and night and people knew that they could find a listening ear, a cup of tea or a bed for the night. But their actions went beyond neighbourliness to an active political engagement to tackle some of the roots of endemic poverty. Geoff Shaw, one of the most prominent members of the group, became the first Convenor of the newly formed Strathclyde Region, working himself ultimately to an early death in his service of the poor of Glasgow. True Godliness can be a costly business.

Breaking Free: Prayer as Repentance

For many years, I was taught to believe that salvation depended on repentance of my sins and on Jesus' forgiveness. It was impressed upon me how totally unworthy we were to receive this forgiveness; so unworthy indeed of God's love that we were totally unable in our own strength to lift ourselves from this pit. Only God's saving grace could do this.

While well aware of my own shortcomings, and firmly believing in God's grace, I do not find this an adequate explanation. There seemed to be an almost competitive need to confess one's faults in order to be worthy of Jesus' love, and an almost obsessive pettiness about the kind of personal transgressions of which one was guilty. The more I questioned this emphasis on personal sin and salvation, the more I began to question the whole theology of the atonement and forgiveness of sin.

As I understand it, the theology is something like this: because of our human condition we are hopelessly flawed, incapable of improving ourselves, and therefore doomed to eternal punishment.

However, because God loves us, he sent his son as a sacrifice to bear the punishment of sin in our place. As a result, not through our own merit, we would have such love for Christ that we would be reconciled to God.

There seem to me to be some basic inconsistencies right at the heart of this theology. If God created us as fallible human beings, destined to fail, and then punished us for this failing, how could this really be a God of love? And then again, as a God of love, how could the deliberate death of his son be part of the divine plan? The whole concept of atonement, of reconciliation to a God of wrath through sacrifice as a substitute for our sin, is a vestige of primitive religion where sacrifices and burnt offerings were made to propitiate an angry God who could make the crops fail. I find such a belief irreconcilable with my own understanding of God and the Spirit, and indeed of the meaning of the life and death of Jesus.

Matthew Fox's book *Original Blessing* came as a breath of fresh air to me, as did the concept of "that of God in everyone". It made far more sense to me that if we carried the image of God within us, then that image was essentially good and creative and full of potential blessing. Robert Barclay's well-loved passage captures some of this idea of the good within us:

> For, when I came into the silent assemblies of God's people,
> I felt a secret power among them, which touched my heart;
> and as I gave way unto it I found the evil weakening in me
> and the good raised up. (QFP § 19.21)

This passage also acknowledges the potential for evil within each of us. One only needs to read the newspapers or to be aware of human history to know the depths of depravity and brutality to which human beings can sink. I do not and cannot, however, believe that this is the natural inherent human condition, nor that such evil can be the will of God.

Having said that, I do not in any way underestimate the power of sin and evil in the world and my own complicity in it. The Iona

Community's morning prayers of confession say, "We confess that our lives, the lives of others, and the life of the world are broken by my sin" (Iona 2001). The fact that the life of the world is broken by my sin was borne in upon me forcibly in Vietnam, where I could see at first hand the horrors of war and the destruction and despoliation of the lives and culture of a whole people in the interests of corporate business and political ambition.

Soon after my return from Vietnam, I was very much influenced by a book by the Baptist minister Ron Sider, *Rich Christians in an Age of Hunger*. In it he speaks of corporate sin and the ways in which our whole lifestyle in the rich countries of the north and west is inevitably bound up with the suffering of the poor.

This seems so relevant to today's world. No matter what we do, our whole way of life in the western world is bound up with past or present exploitation and murder, and in that sense we are all inextricably bound up in corporate guilt. My middle-class upbringing in Glasgow, with all the benefits of a good education, health care and reasonable prosperity, was the end result of Glasgow's history as a city that grew rich on tobacco, shipbuilding and the slave trade. My taxes now pay for Trident, Britain's weapons of mass destruction, which are deployed to "defend Britain's interests anywhere in the world," as defence minister Malcolm Rifkind once told us. These interests are the economic controls that allow me to drive my car, take cheap air flights, wear cheap clothes, buy whatever I want whenever I want it in the supermarkets, all at the expense of the poor.

Tolstoy once said, "I sit on a man's back choking him to death and all the while persuading myself that I am doing everything in my power to help him – except getting off his back."

There is a kind of karmic quality to this cycle of violence and oppression into which we are inevitably trapped by nature of our birth. So is Calvinist theology right? Are we indeed living in such a fallen world that our salvation is impossible and we are surely doomed? At a lecture in Stirling University, I heard the theologian

Jürgen Moltmann say, "Nuclear disaster is a possibility; ecological disaster is a certainty." We may indeed be living in the "end times".

Heaven may exist on earth and may be of our own making, but hell most certainly does exist now in an obscenely real way for millions of people. And hell is also of our own making. There is a logical school of thought that says that precisely because of the fallen nature of our world, we must live with the evils of it, put up with the arms race, the poverty, nuclear weapons and injustice until that day when God's kingdom comes on earth – and that day is not yet.

Or there is a theology that prays the Lord's Prayer for the here and now. "Your kingdom come – *now*", "on earth as in heaven – *now*". That certainly seems to be made explicit in the next part of the prayer, "Give us *this day* our daily bread." Not give me, give us, and not tomorrow, but *this day*, thus acknowledging that the way out of corporate sin is corporate loving and sharing – now.

Thus a prayer for forgiveness of sin is a prayer to enable us to live our lives in a radically different way in the present kingdom – or commonwealth – of God. To live as if another way, free from the trammels and values that trap us in the corporate world of greed, is not only a desirable hope for the future, but is actually possible here and now. This surely is what George Fox meant when he spoke of living "in the virtue of that life and power that takes away the occasion of all wars" (QFP § 24.01).

So the answer to our prayers of repentance lies in essentially practical lifestyle choices. By our actions, however small and insignificant they may seem, we are witnessing to another way of being, to the whole liberating possibility of opting out of the power of sin and into the commonwealth of good.

It is such action, such visible living of another way, that is at the heart of our testimonies – to Truth, Simplicity, the Environment, Justice, Equality and Peace. And the profession of these testimonies is not mere words. The answer to earnest prayer for justice and peace finds its expression in a whole range of activities, from ethical investment to withholding taxes; from buying fairly traded goods to boycotting companies; from befriending asylum seekers to blockading military bases.

In such deeds of resistance we are declaring our total liberation, our recognition of another authority and a higher law. Many of us have an inbuilt resistance to the words "Jesus is Lord", but it is worth remembering that for oppressed people, or people like ourselves enslaved to the structures of violence, these words recognise a different allegiance and a different lordship. It is a question of alignment and of where we take our stance.

A Burning in the Bones: Prayer as Resistance

The uncomfortable, unexpected and exacting aspect of prayer is that once we open ourselves to the Spirit, there is no knowing where she will lead us. I often wonder if we really know how dangerous meeting for worship is. By making ourselves totally open to the working of the Spirit, by reaching down beyond our deepest selves to the very ground of our being, who knows what may happen? We are in effect offering a blank cheque of our lives. This may lead us in directions we had never dreamed of, to new challenges and new ways of living adventurously. Those who think that worship in meeting will give them a quiet life may be in for a surprise.

It is this kind of prayer that breaks us out of the cycle of apathy, despair and helplessness, to acts of prophetic resistance we never knew we were capable of.

So what is it that moves and inspires people to venture beyond their safe world into new paths? The words of an Iona Community hymn offer some clue: "Inspired by love and anger; disturbed by need and pain" (Iona 2001). Many are inspired to action by a profound love of their fellow humans and a deep pity for the world's suffering. It was this kind of love that caused Jesus to weep over Jerusalem and John Woolman to campaign tirelessly against slavery, or which gave George Fox his vision on Pendle Hill of a multitude waiting to be gathered.

We are often more comfortable with love as a motive for action, but all too often we dilute love into something rather vague and insipid, not carrying the strength of steel at its heart. St Augustine wrote, "Hope has two daughters: Anger and Courage", and Allan Boesak, writing in the context of apartheid South Africa wrote:

> We lack a holy rage. The recklessness which comes from
> the knowledge of God and humanity. The ability to rage
> when justice lies prostrate on the streets and when the lie
> rages across the face of the earth. A holy anger about things
> that are wrong with the world. To rage against the ravaging
> of God's earth and the destruction of God's world. To rage
> when little children must die of hunger while the tables of
> the rich are sagging with food. To rage against the senseless
> killing of so many and against the madness of militarism.
> To rage at the lie that calls the threat of death and the strategy
> of destruction "peace". To rage against the complacency of so
> many in the church who fail to see that we shall live only by
> the truth, and that our fear will be the death of us all...
> To restlessly seek that recklessness that will challenge, and
> to seek to change human history until it conforms to the
> norms of the kingdom of God (Boesak 1984).

This surely is the kind of holy anger that is the other side of the coin of love. While anger can be a negative, destructive, consuming force, it can also be the vital transforming spark that moves us out of our apathy. Perhaps the tempering factor is how we channel that anger, and whether it is sincerely motivated by love.

A personal tale I often tell took place on the Island of Mull on a beautiful summer's day. It was one of those perfect Hebridean days, the sea sparkling in the sunlight, distant islands a blue haze on the horizon, bees bumming in the heather. I was reading about Buddhist teaching on non-attachment. Suddenly I stood up, plunged my arms into a bank of heather and said out loud, "But I am attached, I'm passionately attached." I care passionately about the planet, the environment in which I live, the people around me. Passion is the mainspring of my action, and a glorious part of the life force in me.

Passion is such a significant word. It can describe the very heights of joy and ecstasy, but it also holds suffering, pain and loss. The Buddhists are right that any close attachment holds within it the seeds of its own destruction, and the grief and sadness of inevitable loss. But for my part, I would choose the passion, well aware of its full significance and its potential for suffering.

There is a parable told of a person arriving at the judgement seat, and being asked, "Where are your wounds?" When the supplicant admits to being unscathed and bearing no wounds, the question comes, "Was there nothing worth fighting for?" [24] It is precisely at this point of passionate love and anger that prayer becomes resistance. This is the prayer of the prophets; it is uncomfortable, difficult to live with, and almost all the prophets of the past resisted and struggled against it. Jeremiah described his call to action as a fire burning in the bones, irresistible and all-consuming.

It is interesting to note how often fire appears in these descriptions of the prophetic call: Moses recognising the presence of the divine in a burning bush; the first disciples cowering in fear, being touched by tongues of fire and a mighty rushing wind. Surely this is the same prophetic fire that we experience in meeting, when the mouth goes dry, the hands become clammy and the heart beats unbearably quickly as we are reluctantly pushed to ministry.

However we describe it, this driving force is irresistible and pushes us out of our comfort zone into action. "I can no other, here I stand."

There is a poem from a Christian CND leaflet which conveys something of the dynamic irresistibility of that prophetic wind and fire:

> You can't stop that wind you can't kill that fire.
> That wind is the wind of truth, that fire is the fire of love

and that wind keeps right on blowing and that fire keeps
    right on burning.

You Citizens of Century Twenty AD
you can't stop that wind you can't kill that fire
you can chant your creeds as you kill one another
you can flaunt your guns in the face of truth

but you cannot kill the fire of love you cannot stop the
    wind of truth
and when you sense your coldness and when your fear fills
    you with emptiness
that wind will gently breathe new life into your soul
that fire will fan to life the flame of love.

Herein is liberation and freedom from the shackles of sin that
we spoke of in the last chapter. It is a standing up against the forces
of oppression and injustice and saying "*No pasarán!*", putting our
bodies, our talents, our skills, efforts however small and feeble they
may seem, against the system. It is vital here to acknowledge and
celebrate the variety of ways of taking action, not only the media-
catching events, but also the countless, seemingly insignificant
actions carried out, often at great personal cost.

When Ellen and I were starting up Stirling CND we received a
letter from a woman called Janey, who wanted to join. She told us
that she was dying of cancer and only had a few months to live, but
she wanted to be involved. So she wrote letters to the papers and to
MPs on behalf of the group, right up to the week of her death.

And then there was Rita, stiff with arthritis, who faithfully
delivered leaflets for the World Disarmament Campaign to people
living in Glasgow tenements, toiling up and down flights of stairs,
on her own, after dark.

And the countless people who make the big decision to take
part in their first-ever demonstration. For all these people, some
other influence, beyond simply their friends or the urging of some

campaign organiser, moves them to take that extra step beyond what is safe or comfortable.

When HMS *Vanguard*, the first Trident submarine, arrived on the Clyde in 1991, many protestors gathered by the shore in their canoes and small boats. I was in a single canoe, fully expecting to be arrested almost at once, but by some strange oversight the police never spotted me and I was able to paddle to the other side of the loch unnoticed. Somewhat to my horror I realised that there was nothing to stop me paddling my canoe in front of it. There looming in front of me was the huge black bulk of the submarine, epitomising all that we had struggled against for the past fifteen years. As I paddled round in circles trying to decide what to do next, I had a strong feeling of being pushed, propelled forward by a kind of "communion of saints" – George MacLeod, of the Iona Community; Roger Gray, an indomitable peace activist from Skye who had died some years before; Reg Comley, my dear activist friend who was dying in hospital. I felt myself to be in a kind of bubble with all of them urging me forward saying, "What's keeping you? Don't turn back now." As I started paddling towards the bows, a boatload of marines came racing up and stopped me. I was enormously relieved, but I have never forgotten that feeling of compulsion.

Sometimes, however, discerning the movement of the Spirit is not so spontaneous, but involves hard and difficult wrestling with the issues. The request from Trident Ploughshares for the Quaker Turning the Tide programme to train its activists presented Friends with a very hard challenge. Trident Ploughshares was basing its actions on the International Court of Justice ruling in July 1996 that nuclear weapons were contrary to international humanitarian law. As the UK government was still deploying Trident in contravention of international law, Trident Ploughshares was urging citizens to take responsibility themselves by safely, accountably and nonviolently dismantling the submarines or related facilities. Turning the Tide was asked to provide the nonviolence training.

Obviously the activists would be involved not only in civil disobedience but also in property damage of a fairly high order, and thus Friends were presented with a real dilemma. To many the idea of property damage seemed violent; there was a serious possibility that Friends' charitable status might be brought into question, endangering other good work, and law-breaking of this kind might be seen as playing into the hands of extremists.

On the other hand there was the undoubted commitment and integrity of the Trident Ploughshares pledgers, many of whom were Friends; there was the clear imperative of international law; and there was the unchanging nature of the Peace Testimony: "We utterly deny all outward wars and strife" (QFP § 24.04). Turning the Tide felt that the whole credibility of "our testimony to the whole world" was in the balance. Meeting for Sufferings wrestled hard and long with the issue. Eventually they reached a landmark decision, and many who were present at the meeting said that they felt a strong conviction of the Spirit moving them at that time.

There is no doubt that prophetic action is costly. A Quaker Peace and Service poster says, "Let us take the risks of peace upon ourselves and not impose the risks of war on others." Opposing the structures of power, oppression and exploitation is dangerous. It can mean loss of friends, job, status, health, even life itself. But it is just such actions of visible risk-taking that move people to change. So many of the great changes in history have been brought about by the example of committed prophetic actions. "More things are wrought by prayer than this world dreams of," wrote Tennyson, but it is often the outward expression of prayer in action which actually effects the change. Images stay with us: the lone figure in front of the tank at Tiananmen Square, Suffragettes chained to the railings, Dorothy Day sitting quietly on her stool confronting the police, the Committee of 100 members in Trafalgar Square.

I am convinced that over the years of our anti-nuclear demonstrating there has been a positive shift of perception in our favour. When I was in prison for the first time, I was somewhat apprehensive of the kind of reception I might receive from the other women prisoners. I was amazed by the warmth of their response and their immediate understanding of why I was there. "You're doing this for all our children," said one. Rather more recently, during the French testing of nuclear weapons in the Pacific, I was on a flight home from the USA. When the air hostess asked if I preferred red or white wine, I asked if the wine was French. "Oh no, madam," was her reply. "Our customers wouldn't allow it."

In his nonviolence trainings, George Lakey, the well-known US activist, describes one stage of a nonviolent campaign strategy as "propaganda of the deed": the kind of symbolic actions that raise people's awareness of the issues at stake and bring these matters to the forefront of the political agenda. Perhaps that is just another way of describing prophetic action.

The Precious Habitation: Prayer as a Way of Being

In some contrast perhaps to the last chapter, there is a very real sense in which prayer can be simply a state of being – of being in relation to time, of being right with God, of relaxing into the knowledge of being in the right place.

Some of this undoubtedly comes through the sheer joy and wonder at the beauty of nature and the world around us, and is expressed in gratitude and exuberance, in a wonderful sense of all creation singing and rejoicing. To quote the poetry of the prophet Isaiah:

> For you shall go out in joy,
>   and be led back in peace;
> the mountains and the hills before you
>   shall burst into song,
> and all the trees of the field shall clap their hands.

(Isaiah 55:12, New RSV)

Music, art and poetry too convey this sense of wonder and awareness of a music beyond ourselves. I never cease to be thrilled when the long-drawn-out chords of the slow movement of Beethoven's Emperor Concerto suddenly erupt in the sheer exuberance of the third movement; my spirit dances in a blaze of orange and gold with van Gogh's sunflowers; and the precisely honed beauty of my own brother's poetry often moves me to tears. Even the sheer exhilaration of dancing a really lively Eightsome Reel at a ceilidh; these are all, I believe, expressions of an attitude of prayer – of glorying in the gift of life and giving thanks to the Giver. When I am asked where I get my sustenance for the long haul of working for peace, I know that these are some of the wells from which I drink.

Our daughter Marian has difficulty expressing herself verbally, possibly as a result of her experiences in Vietnam. Hence the idea of praying with words would not be part of her experience. However, she radiates a wonderful sense of calm and intuitiveness, and many people who came to Peace House said that Marian's quiet presence in the room enriched their whole experience.

The value of silence as a place of sustaining and upholding at the very deepest of levels has been recognised throughout the ages. Jesus, Muhammed, the Buddha and the prophets all retreated from time to time to a place of quiet. Taking time on one's own every day to find a place of stillness, sitting quietly with one or two friends in unspeaking communion, experiencing the profound depth of a centred meeting, or sitting in that palpable stillness of 2000 Friends gathered at Yearly Meeting: all of these are places to listen to the "still, small voice of calm".

In the convent of San Marco in Florence there is a painting by Piero Della Francesca which depicts Jesus standing on trial before Caiaphas the High Priest. An aura of stillness and quiet surrounds the solitary figure, conveying a wonderful sense of calm and dignity. There can be a sense even in the midst of the whirlwind and the storm, in the very heat of the action, of standing calmly in the right place. In a video of the anti-globalisation protests in Seattle in 1999 one image stays in my mind. It is of a tall young man standing in an attitude of prayer with tear gas swirling all around. Eventually driven to his knees by the choking gas, he remains in prayer, a solitary, determined, still centre. Ellen says that while she was standing on the deck of the Trident facility in the middle of Loch Goil, throwing one computer after another to the bottom of the loch, she experienced not only powerful exhilaration, but also an absolute sense of calm and the "rightness" of her actions.

Her actions inevitably led to a period of time in prison on remand for four and a half months and this was one of the hardest times in our lives. It even included a threat of eviction from our cottage, and yet we both agreed that we were enveloped in an underlying feeling of good. Some kind of purpose was being worked out through her actions and my support, that was not only going to have far-reaching implications for the peace movement, but which was at the same time offering us comfort and sustenance.

Throughout my life I have been blessed with a strong sense of being guided, sustained and upheld; of engaging in a thrilling adventure, which has brought me some of the greatest happiness and staunchest friendships I could know. Perhaps when the Psalmist writes of "dwelling in the house of the Lord for ever" (Psalm 23:6), this is the same as the "precious habitation" of which John Woolman speaks (QFP § 20.10). Of course there are times of doubt, of questioning; there is always the admonition "Think it possible you might be mistaken" (QFP § 1.02 no. 17); but there is an overall sense of direction and purpose that gives comfort and courage.

So what of the times in our lives when that direction changes: when we are no longer able to be so active, when we retire, or when new challenges and different opportunities suggest a change of direction? For some retirement, redundancy or a change of direction can be a real trauma. Often one's personal identity and feelings of self-worth are so closely bound up with one's daily job or occupation that when change comes, it can be a very demoralising,

difficult time. It is at such times of letting go, of having the confidence
to allow others to take over one's dreams, that prayer or a sense of
right direction becomes so important.

I have reached just such a point in my life now. It became very
clear to me that I should retire at the age of 60. In some ways this was
quite a hard decision, as the Scottish Centre for Nonviolence which
I had started in 1999 was at a moment of crisis, urgently needing
funding and yet just on the edge of breakthrough to interesting new
developments. On the other hand, I was conscious of being tired,
somewhat jaded, lacking in enthusiasm, even damping people's
ardour with the fatal words, "Oh we tried that before and it didn't
work." There was no doubt at all in my mind that it was time to go.
Not only that, there could be no looking back. I had to leave my
successor absolute freedom to change direction, throw things out,
pursue a totally different course, without my intervention.

The amazing tale of our move to the north-west of Scotland is
already told. Now that we are settled here in an idyllic spot, quiet,
lovely, we feel at ease, relaxed, totally calm. In the right place in fact.

But are we deluding ourselves? Is the decision to live in a
beautiful isolated spot not just sheer escapism? What of our pledge
as Trident resisters, what of the Rule of the Iona Community to
work for justice and peace, what about the Peace Testimony?
Have we renounced all these commitments, turned our backs on
involvement and retreated to a pleasant little Nirvana of our own?

Somehow I am convinced that this is not so. We have to
acknowledge that there comes a time to do things differently. An
acknowledgement that there can be different ways of being engaged
that are every bit as significant and effective as demonstrating,
protesting and being "in the forefront of the action". There is a time
to hand over to younger, more energetic people; a time to realise
that the world does not depend on our actions alone; a time of
letting go, of waiting to see where the path will lead us next. One
thing is certain, after so many amazing so-called coincidences, we
are quite sure that we are meant to be where we are and that there

is a purpose for us. It may be that the peace of our home can give a welcome to tired activists; it may be that it is time to reflect and write about our experiences and record some of the often forgotten history of the peace movement; it may be that simply our own quiet way of "being present" may be of help to others – or is this time of quiet the calm before the storm, the ante-chamber to our next big adventure? We wait with eagerness.

In previous sections of this book I have explored in a very personal way what prayer means to me, some of the ways in which prayer happens and how prayer has informed my activism. In the next section I will begin to explore some of the underlying questions. Whom are we praying to? How does this relate to a belief in God? In what ways are our actions empowered by the Spirit? What is the nature of power? What about success and failure? I will be writing from the perspective of my own Christian upbringing and conviction, but hopefully doing so in a way that sheds new light and a different perspective.

Part Three *Bedrock of Faith*

A Cupboard of Delights

Over my years of struggling with questions of faith, I have developed a metaphor that I have found helpful. I visualise a cupboard full of the exciting goodies of my faith. The things that I use a lot, necessary commodities, are on the middle shelf, about eye level, well within reach, ready to be pulled out and used every day. Some things are out of reach on the top shelf, probably useful at some time in the future, but not particularly helpful at the moment. These are the points of faith that I can't understand, but I know instinctively that they may need to be brought down, dusted off and re-examined sometime. On the bottom shelf are the things that are going to be thrown out as worthless or even harmful. The important thing is that items of faith can be moved around every time I tidy the cupboard and re-examine its contents, while there is always room on the shelves for more.

In the chapter which follows, I will be exploring some of these tenets of belief that I have found vitally necessary as an underpinning for my active life. Of course there will be huge omissions and my choices are the product of my own subjectivity: not a museum piece of polished exhibits or final answers, but simply an invitation to explore.

Ground of Our Being or Ancient of Days?

All that has been written so far is based on the premise that there is a God, who exists beyond ourselves and therefore gives prayer a meaning. But is this so? How do we experience God and to what extent does God in any way answer our prayers or inspire our actions?

John Robinson's book *Honest to God* and some of the writings of Teilhard de Chardin and Paul Tillich had a profound influence on the way people of my generation thought about God. John Robinson challenged the whole concept of an all-powerful father figure, dwelling in a far-off heaven, able to dispense justice and intervene dramatically in the affairs of human life. The "immortal, invisible, God only wise", the "Ancient of Days, pavilioned in splendour and girded with praise" spoken of in the hymn books.

Belief in such a God must certainly influence the way we pray. Often it leads to a huge sense of inadequacy, of total unworthiness and shame before such splendour and might, so that abasing oneself in confession of sins becomes a prerequisite to prayer. From this comes the need for an intermediary, priest, minister, an advocate before God, who is in some way more holy, more inspired, more endowed with grace, who can plead our cause.

There is also inevitably a strong element of fear, leading to a timidity and reluctance to step out of line, to act out of turn, to challenge the religious authorities and in any way incur the wrath of God. This can lead to a kind of social and moral conservatism.

By extension, belief in a God of such certainties can lead to a sense of over-riding moral rectitude, a conviction of the rightness of one's cause to the exclusion of all others, and a clear-cut idea of right and wrong. There is no room for doubt, and questioning suggests disobedience or even blasphemy.

It is amazing how deeply rooted in our whole culture is this idea of an awe-inspiring patriarchal, transcendent God, and how embedded in our psyche is the idea of a male, dominant and often vengeful God. This is precisely the kind of notion of God that feminists would reject as exemplifying all that is negative and abusive in patriarchal structures. A friend of mine recently spoke about her great difficulty in reading the Bible at all, describing much of it as "toxic waste", fit only to be thrown out. And quite right too. This is the Lord of Hosts, the God of Battles, the Conquering King in whose name wars can be fought, imperial conquest justified, and whose name can be used as a battle-cry in the midst of slaughter. This is the angry God who punishes sin with horrible savagery, an all-pervasive seeing eye who pursues us relentlessly like the hound of hell.

In his book *Jesus Against Christianity*, Jack Nelson-Pallmeyer points out that most of us are highly selective in our reading of the

Bible, and carefully edit out the over-riding picture of a God who is pathologically violent. We focus on the hope of the rainbow, conveniently ignoring that a flood, apparently masterminded by God, had wiped out nearly all of humanity. We read Exodus as a story of the liberation of oppressed people, not noticing that Egyptian slaves were also the victims of all the plagues, including the killing of the firstborn children. We sing merrily about the walls of Jericho falling down, overlooking a programme of genocide that appeared to have divine approval. God as portrayed in much of the Bible is ruthless, vengeful, arbitrary and genocidal. Pallmeyer claims that we ignore this aspect of the Bible at our peril.

Although many of us at an intellectual level have rejected this image of God, vestiges of such attitudes remain and are surprisingly deep-seated even in our secular society, and might be said to underpin many of our western values of supremacy today.

I have always struggled with belief in a transcendent God precisely because I find this so hard to reconcile with a God of love. But if we dismiss totally the idea of a God "out there", beyond ourselves, all-seeing, all-wise, guiding and directing our actions, we must find a new location for God. If I still believe in God, still believe that there is a greater purpose beyond my own ends, still believe in divine guidance from a source beyond myself, then where is this God, and in what ways is this God different from the "Ancient of Days"?

Much of the problem centres around whether our belief is in a transcendent God "out there" or an immanent God discovered in the depths of our being. For Friends, of course, this is not a new debate.

Personally, I derive much more comfort and inspiration in the idea of a God who is "closer than breathing", the very ground of our being. This shifts the entire focus of the divine away from distant inaccessibility, to an immediate immanent presence within every one of us, constantly present and constantly loving. Thus, not only is God the very essence and core of my own being, there is also "that of God" in every person I meet. The Nepalese greeting *Namaste*, usually coupled with a folding of the hands and a bow, means "The God within me greets the God within you".

There is a direct connection between a belief in this kind of God and the respect that forms the whole basis of nonviolence. If every one of us embodies an aspect of the truth of God, the divine, the very essence of humanity, then this must immediately affect how we treat that person. This was at the heart of Gandhi's teaching. If we kill or use violence against another human being, then we are doing violence to the truth of God within them.

Even enemies, those with whom we profoundly disagree, have this element of the divine, and it becomes our task to seek that out in order to be able to move forward in mutual respect. Nonviolent action is based on the assumption that by one's own actions, by confronting people openly and lovingly in a new and creative way, one can reach this deep inner core of the divine, appeal to the very highest nature within a person and so effect change. And of course the change may need to happen within oneself. This is why part of nonviolence training teaches one to look one's opponent in the eye, thus encountering the window on the soul, meeting as human to human and saying, "You cannot ignore my humanity, just as I respect yours". And of course this is also one of the reasons why secret police wear visors and dark glasses, precisely to avoid such a deeply challenging contact.

At the start of the Options for Defence week on Iona, during which military generals, military experts and peace campaigners gathered for a conference, we all assembled in the Chapter House of the Abbey. It was a distinctly stiff beginning, suspicion in the air and each side eyeing the other with proverbial hackles raised. To begin the introductions and attempt to ease the atmosphere, I said that we all sincerely believed that we were working for peace, but simply differed over the methods. The relief was almost palpable as shoulders came down, people relaxed into their seats and began to look each other in the eye.

I remember an occasion at the peace camp at Greenham Common. We had been blockading a gate for several hours, when a decision was made to open the gates forcibly from the inside by driving at them with a large truck. The gates were being forced open slowly and women were being crushed under the gate as it swung. Those of us lined up on the outside, hemmed in by a solid row of police, felt totally helpless and at a loss as to what to do. Eventually we decided to stand up and speak to the police officer directly in front of each one of us. I was opposite a very young man, and as I was angry and distressed I said, rather unkindly, "Do you like doing this kind of thing?" To my consternation his eyes filled with tears and he said, "I am hating every minute of it and I wish I was anywhere else."

Of course there are times when it seems impossible to discern that of God in the other; times when all appeals fail and attempts to make peace can lead to suffering and even death. Yet unbelievably, in some of the most extreme situations there are amazing stories of how the deep humanity of another has been touched and a seemingly horrific situation transformed.

There is a remarkable book by a man called Eric Lomax, who was a prisoner of the Japanese during the Second World War. He experienced horrific torture at the hands of his captors, and one man in particular was to haunt his nightmares for years after the end of the war. He visited psychiatrists and medical experts, but to no avail. Eventually he realised that he must force himself to come face to face with this man and speak with him about what had happened and, if possible, find it in himself to extend forgiveness. It took him many years of searching, but at last he discovered that the man who had been his torturer had been so haunted with guilt for what he had done that he had entered a Japanese monastery, and that he too was seeking out his victim to seek forgiveness. In a painfully honest but very moving scene the book describes how the two men eventually met and were able to give each other release and peace of mind.

This illustrates a belief in God who at the core of our humanity goes beyond the confines of our individual human experience to include a dynamic within the whole universe. One of my main reasons for believing in some kind of divine purpose comes from the sheer wonder and beauty of creation. Where we live in the far north-west of Scotland we are privileged to be able to enjoy the darkness, and even occasionally the wonder of the Northern Lights. Seeing great curtains of light flickering like searchlights in a great canopy across the sky, or pausing to reflect on the time it has taken for the light of an individual star to reach our tiny planet, makes me so aware of how infinitesimally small we are in the whole cosmos.

Or at the other end of the spectrum, consider the tiny magic of a seed unfurling in the warm earth, or the little interlocking feathers of a wren, or the green brushes of a larch in spring, or the minute perfection of a sea shell, and wonder at the beauty of it all. In that sense I cannot but believe in a creator, not so much as initiating an organised act of creation, but as a purpose for good behind the universe. "And God saw that it was very good." As the letter attributed to Chief Seattle says, "To harm the earth is to heap contempt on its Creator."

I am not a scientist and confess profound ignorance of the finer points of chaos theory and the physics of the universe, but I have a vivid memory of being shown a video at Woodbrooke, the Quaker study centre in Birmingham, which showed computerised images of fractals, explained for the lay person. Seemingly random objects such as forests, clouds or mountain ranges were programmed into the computer in such a way as to show the most amazing patterns and designs. I was profoundly moved and thrilled, as it seemed to me to show a design for life far beyond our understanding, full of sheer beauty.

It is this love of the environment that we live in, and of the infinite variety of people around me, that inspires in me a deep reverence and gratitude for life, and so moves me to action.

My understanding of God, then, could be described as being in the connectedness of all life. God for me is like the divine spark that links me to another human being, to the animals, to all of creation – a kind of great web of connection, alive, shimmering with energy, creating flashes of inspiration and profound love.

In his profound book *I and Thou*, philosopher Martin Buber makes a distinction between the ordinary relationship of I/it and the numinous spiritual meeting of I/Thou. Saying that "In the beginning is relation" and that "All real living is meeting", he describes the encounter with the "Thou". "The *Thou* meets me. But I step into direct relation with it. Hence the relation means being chosen and choosing, suffering and action in one." In a remarkable passage he describes the different encounters in relation to a tree.

> I consider a tree.
> I can look on it as a picture: stiff column in a shock of light, or splash of green shot with the delicate blue and silver of the background.
> I can perceive it as movement: flowing veins on clinging, pressing pith, suck of the roots, breathing of the leaves, ceaseless commerce with earth and air – and the obscure growth itself.
> I can classify it in a species and study it as a type in its structure and mode of life…
> In all this the tree remains my object, occupies space and time, and has its nature and constitution.
> It can, however, also come about, if I have both will and grace, that in considering the tree I become bound up in relation to it. The tree is no longer *It*. I have been seized by the power of exclusiveness… Everything belonging to the tree is in this: its form and structure, its colours and chemical composition, its intercourse with the elements and with the stars, all are present in a single whole.

Buber describes this unique relationship as universal love and calls it the "cradle of Real Life".

In a somewhat similar way, Buddhist philosophy teaches that we have more than five senses; that there is what is called the *aliya* consciousness behind all the other senses which is the sense that makes the connection enabling us to see, hear and touch reality. Thus prayer becomes a way of plugging into this web of connection, of living and being in tune with the dance of the spheres that is both part of our own inner consciousness, while at the same time being part of a goodness infinitely beyond our imagining.

Reaching Beyond Ourselves

Looking back into the past and even into our own lives, there are times when people seem to accomplish deeds, perform acts of heroism, undertake projects that are totally unexpected and far beyond their own seeming limitations and powers. Very often this is ascribed to a power or dynamism beyond our own experience and external to our own imaginings.

Where does that "still, small voice" come from, tugging at the heartstrings, annoyingly imperative and brooking no refusal? So often the voice of conscience is obviously not in our own best interests at the time, leading us inexorably to places we are afraid of or where we would rather not be. I remember travelling on the train from Glasgow to London en route for my two years in Vietnam and the adventure of a lifetime. I was homesick already and had tears pouring down my cheeks, when a woman sitting opposite leaned across and patted my arm saying, "Yes dear, London is a long way from home!"

History is filled with inspiring examples of people who have done amazing things, well beyond their ordinary powers. I often quote a poem by Adrienne Rich which has become one of my favourites:

My heart is moved by all I cannot save:
so much has been destroyed
I have to cast my lot with those
who age after age, perversely,
with no extraordinary power,
reconstitute the world.

(Rich 1978)

However, I would take issue with the line "with no extraordinary power". People do sometimes appear to act out of some sort of "extraordinary power".

Jesus' disciples, for example, were as ordinary a bunch of characters as you could find. James and John arguing over pride of place; Peter, rash and impetuous, blustering and vehement in his denials; Matthew the money-grubbing tax collector and collaborator; Thomas the cynical doubter: all of them taking flight at the critical moment of testing and cowering fearfully in the upper room, jumping at the first knock at the door. And yet this same group of country peasants were able to stand up publicly and proclaim what they had experienced, in direct defiance of all the might of the religious and military establishment. They scattered all over the Roman Empire, in and out of prison, finding an eloquence and courage far beyond themselves.

Some years ago I was attending a week on Iona led by Vincent Harding, a theologian from the US who had worked alongside Martin Luther King. I had been asked to lead the worship in the Abbey that evening, and I asked Vincent to read Dr King's description of his experience of being in the depths of despair. It was during the Montgomery bus boycott, and he had just received a threatening abusive telephone call in the middle of the night. He wrote:

It seemed that all my fears had come down on me at once.
I had reached the saturation point...I was ready to give up.
I tried to think of a way to move out of the picture without

appearing to be a coward. In this state of exhaustion, when my courage had almost gone, I determined to take my problem to God. My head in my hands, I bowed over the kitchen table and prayed aloud ... At that moment I experienced the presence of the Divine as I had never before experienced him. It seemed as though I could hear the quiet assurance of an inner voice saying, "Stand up for righteousness, stand up for truth, God will be at your side forever." Almost at once my fears began to pass from me. My uncertainty disappeared. I was ready to face anything. The outer situation remained the same, but God had given me inner calm.

Three nights later, our home was bombed. Strangely enough, I accepted the word of the bombing calmly. My experience with God had given me a new strength and trust.

(King 1963)

Vincent read the passage aloud in the Abbey with the tears streaming down his face. After the service he handed the book back to me and told me that he had been with Dr King the morning after that experience and had been told the whole story.

So people do experience an enabling power, which many would attribute to God or the Spirit working within them. Some would call it the power of Jesus, and I would like to explore this theme a little further.

As I have already mentioned, I was brought up an enthusiastic Christian and a church member. On my return from Vietnam, I was no longer so certain. I had experienced other faiths and philosophies and learned much from them. I was also appalled by the arrogance of some western Christians. However, I was living in Scotland, in a culture that was ostensibly Christian, so I continued to describe myself as Christian mainly out of cultural conformity, but also because the example of Jesus' life still gave me an inspirational pattern to aspire to. Joining Friends gave me the freedom to explore my spirituality in a supportive, non-judgemental environment.

However, during a bible-study role play on Iona, I came to experience something profoundly revealing about the power which Jesus had which has remained with me ever since as a challenge and an inspiration.

The passage which we were studying was from Matthew's Gospel, the story of the paralysed man being lowered through the roof by his friends for Jesus to heal. We were a large group of about 40 people, and we began by reading the passage through carefully. We were then offered a choice of groups – a disciples group, the man's friends, a group of "paralysed people", a Pharisees group, onlookers, and a Jesus group. We were encouraged to pick the group that most interested us. I found myself in the Jesus group. Each group was then given a short task to help us into our role. The paralysed people just lay on the floor; the Pharisees were given various legal passages of scripture to study; the Jesus group that I was in was asked to think quickly about what our message to the crowd was going to be.

After we had done this we were given some questions about our characters, and asked specifically to use our imaginations to think about how we were feeling at the time, still in our role as Jesus. My imaginings really surprised me. I found myself thinking that I was young, a bit of a country lad, speaking in a broad local dialect, inexperienced, not at all sure of my authority, and, yes, frightened. Totally real, totally human feelings. And yet completely at odds with all I had previously believed about Jesus as "Son of God", somehow special, untouched by everyday worries, going through life knowing it would be "all right in the end". Here suddenly was a human being, a frightened, fallible person, just like me. It bowled me over!

Almost immediately in the role play we were given our next task, which was to go over to the Pharisees group and ask them in what way we were causing them offence. By this time we were so afraid that we drew straws for the task, and I was one of two detailed to go. It was like stirring up a hornets' nest! We were bombarded with legalistic jargon about why we should not be healing the man, and we were repeatedly asked the very question we weren't sure about: "On what authority can you do these things?"

We suddenly found ourselves blazingly angry that such legalism could prevent an act of mercy, and we both found ourselves quoting passages of Micah and Amos we had forgotten we ever knew. It was a gloriously liberating experience of holy rage.

As we gathered together to make peace with each other and reflect on what we had learned, I felt as if I had received a profoundly exciting revelation – one which I am still processing today.

Firstly I learned that Jesus was as fully human as I am, subject to all the same joys, fears, triumphs and limitations. In fact Jesus was often described as the "Son of Man", and I had always given this title a somewhat exalted, mystical meaning. But it can be quite simply translated as "the Human One" or "everyman".

But if this Human One, who was like me, was also endowed with special power – was also the Son of God – then by extension I too am a Daughter of God, also able to lay hold of that special power. For a few moments I had experienced a power and outrage beyond myself, and this showed that that special power which Jesus had is also available to me. This is the power that inspired the prophets, Gandhi, Martin Luther King, Rosa Parks, Dorothy Day – and me. It was an extraordinarily exciting discovery.

I went back to the Gospels and read them through again in the light of this discovery, and I found many passages where Jesus seemed to be emphasising this very message to his listeners. He said things like "The kingdom of God is *within you*" (Luke 17:21), or "Greater things shall you do" (John 14:21); he sent the disciples out in pairs in the full expectation that they could carry out his mission just as effectively as he could.

Then I began to reflect on the word "Messiah". Messiah means the "anointed one", and there is a very real sense in which we are all anointed with the Spirit to do the work of the kingdom. "You are the One we have all been waiting for."

This was exciting stuff, and as I tried to explain it to people, just as I am doing here, I discovered the inadequacies of language to express deep spiritual experience. Some friends would say to me, "Oh, so you've been born again", or "You've taken the Lord Jesus Christ as your saviour and lord", and I would react vehemently, "Oh, no, nothing like that." And yet how do I really know what others mean when they use these words, or how do I put my feelings into words?

It sounds supremely arrogant and even blasphemous to say that I can experience the same kind of power as Jesus, and of course it was precisely this very question of authority and source of power that constituted the offence of Jesus to the religious leaders of his time. Such claims led him directly into conflict with church and state.

And this is the sting in the tail. Just as, in the role play, I felt fear when going to speak with the Pharisees, so now it came to me with blinding clarity that claiming this power and letting it drive where it must, leads straight into trouble. As Douglas Steere once said, "A Christian should be without fear, happy and always in trouble"!

Reweaving the Broken Web

Connections can be broken; the web is frail like gossamer. We know from our own experience that relationships are broken, trust betrayed; that goodness and love can be abused, scorned, trampled ruthlessly underfoot. Beauty in nature is being despoiled, ravaged, exploited to the point of extinction and total destruction. Far from being one with the flow of life, all too often we humans seem to have a death wish.

If God is in these connections, then does this mean that God is able to be broken, destroyed? In other words, that God is not omnipotent, all-powerful, able to save the world, but that God is vulnerable, able to be wounded and even destroyed? "He saved others, himself he cannot save," were the mocking words to Jesus as he was dying.

It would indeed seem to be so, and the crucifixion of Jesus would seem to bear this out. Love can indeed be despised, rejected, even put to death.

This concept of a vulnerable God would go some way to answering some of those hard questions about unanswered prayer. There is an irreconcilable gap between a God who is love and a God who is all-powerful. The age-old question arises of how a God of love can allow disasters, tragedies, pain and suffering to happen. If suffering is indeed part of God's will, then God cannot be a God of love. True perhaps that suffering and pain can build character and refine our natures; but that God could will such disasters upon us in order to make us love God more would suggest a warped, self-centred, malevolent God.

On the other hand, a God who wills the good, but who suffers alongside us – is literally com-passionate – is much closer to the God of love in whom I can place my confidence. Where was God when the bomb was dropped on Hiroshima? The answer comes back: "God was in Hiroshima with the suffering people." It seems to me that believing in God's omnipotence can be a real obstacle to prayer, and that when we look at the meaning of power in a new way, we may find some answers.

This understanding of a God who is not all-powerful means that we are rejecting the idea of a puppet-master God who can manipulate events and intervene powerfully in history. Does this then mean that we are also rejecting any idea of a divine purpose at work? I would say not.

As a historian I am fascinated by the unexpectedness of events, the tiny conjunctions of events and circumstances that can change the course of history. It is always good fun to speculate on the "what ifs" of history. However, I do not view history as a series of direct interventions by God, but rather as the result of the committed or sometimes mistaken actions of individual people. The Jewish Passover celebrates God's deliverance of the Jewish people from slavery in Egypt, but Moses' willingness to undertake the task, to overcome his fears, to rise to the challenge of defying the might of Pharaoh, was a crucial part of that deliverance. There is a more indirect intervention in that Moses experienced an encounter with God, which opened his eyes to the suffering of his people, and released his own potential for action. The awareness and compulsion to action may indeed be part of divine inspiration, but for God's purposes to be fulfilled, we ourselves must be prepared to take action. The answer to prayer may be quite simply: "What are you going to do about it?"

Perhaps a more appropriate prayer might be for eyes that see, ears that hear and a heart that cares. "Replace my heart of stone with a heart of flesh", or as a poem by Miriam Teichner puts it:

> God – let me be aware!
> Stab my soul fiercely with others' pain.
> Let me walk seeing horror and stain.
> Let my hands, groping, find other hands.
> Give me the heart that divines, understands,
> Give me the courage, wounded, to fight,
> Flood me with knowledge, drench me with light.
> God – let me be aware!

(Steven 1988)

Many years ago, I came across a poster publicising a meeting of the Christian Union at Glasgow University. It showed a huge nuclear mushroom cloud with the title "Don't worry: God is in charge". I was so incensed that I climbed up on a railing to pull it down, but I would dearly like to have replaced it with a poster saying "Do worry; God is waiting for you to do something."

A passage by Colin Morris quoted in *Anthology of Hope* seems to illustrate the imperative to do something beyond mere words:

In the late 1950s when Britain was preparing to explode
her first hydrogen bomb in the Pacific, the churches yelled
bloody murder, passed frenzied resolutions, protesting,
deploring, expressing grave concern etc, etc, and delegations
of ecclesiastical dignitaries and political pundits waited
on the Prime Minister to threaten and plead. But it was a
60-year-old Unitarian who quietly withdrew his life savings,
bought a little boat and sailed it into the Test Area as his
personal protest. Of course it was idiotic, irresponsible,
quixotic of him, but his action commanded a queer sort of
respect because he was prepared to lay his life on the line for
what he believed.

And we comfortable, well-fed, well-housed soldiers of
Jesus, having made our big speeches and rolled the rhetoric
around our tongues, went to our beds the night the bomb
went off, shaking our heads sadly at the turn of events and
hoping that someone would listen next time. They didn't and
they won't. For politicians understand this word game, too.
Resolutions and deputations don't frighten them. If anything
gives them unease it is crazy little men who sail right into the
heart of big issues in total disregard for their lives. Such men
are dangerous. The rest of us could not be tamer.

Does the answer to prayer then depend solely on our response,
and if so, what of our failure and apathy? Are we saying that faith
depends on works? What when our human efforts are feeble,
lacking in determination, or just plain fail? This philosophy is surely
a road to despair, as so often our weak efforts are pitted against
forces far more powerful than ourselves, and we rarely see any
result for our efforts.

And what about the times when our actions are misguided or
inappropriate? Is prayer purely subjective? Are we simply praying
to ourselves, directed entirely by our own emotions and feelings,
based on our subjective reading of a situation, which may be in
direct opposition to another's equally strongly held convictions?

In positing a vulnerable God, are we simply reducing God to a human dimension, contained and confined by the limitations of our own mortality and weakness?

Perhaps part of the key to understanding this dilemma is to look more closely at what is meant by power in this context. We speak of a vulnerable God, able to be wounded and broken, and this brokenness has been exemplified in the lives of the saints ever since. Here is no triumphant God conquering all opposition; rather this is a God who "takes his kingdom by entreaty". We are speaking here of a very different kind of power: the power of nonviolence, or the power of love. This is the kind of power that does not dominate or trample others underfoot; it is not imposed from above, but rather is an inner power, that wins others to itself by the strength and appeal of love.

In his classic book *The Power of Nonviolence*, Richard Gregg explores the whole dynamic of this very different kind of power. Calling nonviolence "moral ju-jitsu", Gregg describes how one confronts aggressors by appealing to their humanity with nonviolence in a way which is totally new and unexpected, so different from the normal response of violence that the opponent is momentarily thrown off balance as in ju-jitsu. This dynamic can be replicated on a wider stage involving the state or an institution. Nonviolence is based on the understanding that a ruler's power rests on the consent of the people. If this consent is withdrawn, then ultimately the ruler's power base is totally eroded. If, when faced with nonviolent resistance, the state uses force to regain control, people previously neutral or uninvolved will be so turned against the state and its methods that they will be won over to the side of the protestors. One of the reasons that I became so attracted to the Gandhian principles of nonviolence is that they seem to epitomise the values of the kind of Christianity I had come to believe in, and to embody in action this different kind of power.

It might be helpful at this stage to examine these principles of nonviolence in more detail. Perhaps most important, and most often misunderstood, is that nonviolence is essentially confrontational. It is prepared to resist injustice and wrong wherever it occurs, fearlessly and honestly. In so doing, the nonviolent activist is often perceived as creating disorder, rocking the boat and stirring up trouble.

This was particularly so in apartheid South Africa, where campaigners were often accused of stirring up trouble and violence, while what they were really doing was exposing the massive structural violence of a racist regime. Nonviolence exposes the latent violence of society, by lovingly confronting injustice. This passage by the late Leslie Weatherhead captures something of the strong nature of that love:

> Love in the New Testament is stern and strong and severe and virile. It is not sloppy and sentimental and weak…Love is all the things St Paul described in 1 Corinthians 13, but it has steel in it as well as tears…Love suffers, entreats and endures, and fools think this is weakness. But those who oppose love take up arms against the whole universe.
>
> (Steven 1988)

Secondly, by always seeking an alternative to violence, nonviolence has to be essentially creative and innovative, drawing on the resources of imagination and lateral thinking, and releasing a potential for originality. This creative thinking is not limited to the individual interaction; it is also seeking to build the new society, already living out the vision of the world as it could be. Gandhi spoke of doing practical work as an aspect of nonviolence, and this points to the very practical, physical, hands-on building of the alternative society – realising the vision in down-to-earth ways. The Kingdom is here and now, within our grasp, ours to build and live. It is literally "living in that life and power that takes away the occasion of all wars".

In so doing, nonviolence is always seeking out that of God in the other, ever hopeful of finding the best, never demonising or stereotyping, and always seeing the individual human being behind the mask of uniform or allegiance.

Nonviolence also involves being prepared to accept suffering rather than inflict it on others. We are not speaking here about the glorification of martyrdom, but rather about being realistic about the cost of being different, and the possible, even inevitable consequences, of confronting the powers. In a magnificent passage, Martin Luther King points to the way in which, through the committed acceptance of the costs of nonviolence, ultimately the opponent is won over:

> To our most bitter opponents we say: "We shall match your capacity to inflict suffering by our capacity to endure suffering. We shall meet your physical force with soul force. Do to us what you will, and we shall continue to love you... Send your hooded perpetrators of violence into our community at the midnight hour and beat us and leave us half dead, and we shall still love you. But be ye assured that we will wear you down by our capacity to suffer. One day we shall win freedom, but not only for ourselves. We shall so appeal to your heart and conscience that we shall win *you* in the process, and our victory will be a double victory."
>
> (King 1963)

Finally, and perhaps most exciting of all, nonviolence expects change; indeed it believes that through its actions, change has already begun. This is what makes nonviolence revolutionary and turns the world upside down with a completely different set of values. We will return to this theme when we address the question of resurrection, but in our understanding of prayer, it is vital to understand that this is the power we can plug into: the dynamic, unstoppable power of nonviolent love.

Living the Good News

To many of us brought up in the Christian tradition, the word
"Gospel" has become so familiar that it is almost synonymous
with the word "book". Mark's Gospel, John's Gospel sound almost
like the Book of Mark or the Book of John. But its real meaning of
"Good News" should have us on tiptoe with anticipation, tingling
with hope and looking out for something really exciting. "Behold
I bring you good tidings of great joy, which shall be to all people"
(Luke 2:10, AV).

But what exactly is this good news and what relevance does it
have to our lives? I received some insight into this some years ago
during a short spell in prison.

I had been asked to participate in a BBC religious broadcast
discussing the passage in Luke's Gospel which is sometimes referred
to as Jesus' manifesto for action:

> The Spirit of the Lord is upon me, because he has anointed
> me to bring good news to the poor.
> He has sent me to proclaim release to the captives and
> recovery of sight to the blind, to let the oppressed go free,
> and to proclaim the year of the Lord's favour.
>
> (Luke 4:18–19, New RSV)

I was sitting there in my cell trying to prepare material for the
broadcast and asking "What would be 'good news' for the other
women prisoners on my block?" Obviously the immediate short-
term answer would be freedom – freedom to go home, to go on the
town, to see their families again. But what was the deeper, long-term
meaning of good news? I was at a loss to find words that would have
any meaning for my fellow inmates.

A little while later I was having a chat with the woman in the cell
next door. She was inside for the umpteenth time for being drunk
and disorderly. Somewhat naively, I asked if she wouldn't like to join
Alcoholics Anonymous. "Oh no," she said. "To do that you have to
want to give up the drink." "Don't you want to?" I asked. "To want

to give up drink," she said, "you have to respect yourself, and I don't, and neither does anyone else." I had no words of reply.

Of course it is obvious, the good news for that woman is that she is of value, that she is of infinite worth in the eyes of God, and that the fullness of her life matters. But words and phrases like "Jesus loves you", "You are precious in the eyes of God" become meaningless clichés, mere pious words and platitudes. The only way to tell that woman the good news was for me to treat her with absolute respect.

This has an immediate bearing on all our human relationships and on how we treat others. It is this respect that must be at the heart of all our efforts towards racial justice; it is respect that informs our testimony to equality – not just equality under the law and in our social systems, but equality in the eyes of God. It is that profound respect for the life and potential of another human being that makes us active for peace and passionate in opposition to the weapons of death.

It was this ability to recognise the full potential of the most unlikely individuals that characterised Jesus' life. In Jack Nelson-Pallmeyer's book *Jesus Against Christianity*, he points out that most of the creeds of the churches focus on the birth and death of Jesus while missing out the most important part – what he actually did. He gave Matthew, the money-grubbing collaborator, the chance to be generous and popular; he saw beauty in the actions of a woman of doubtful reputation; he provided an outlet for the exuberance and enthusiasms of Peter. In fact he quite deliberately courted criticism by openly associating with those very people whom the religious establishment least respected.

However, Jesus' actions and life went far beyond simply giving affirmation to people. People are not crucified for being kind to others. Jesus' whole life was lived as an alternative nonviolent window on to God – not the vengeful God of retribution, but a loving, compassionate, merciful God. Nor was the purpose of his life to bring about an apocalyptic end-time of ultimate punishment for sins. He set an example of how life might be lived right now in the context of a loving, caring community. What Ron Sider describes as "communities of loving defiance".[51]

Because defiance is exactly what such a lifestyle entails. We can view Jesus' whole ministry as a life lived in deliberate opposition to the domination of his time. It was not enough to show compassion for the poor and dispossessed; the whole system of oppression which left people in poverty and despair had to be challenged. In Jesus' time the domination system was the Roman Empire, founded and maintained by ruthless conquest, and supported by a collaborationist system of client kings such as the Herod family, and religious officials from High Priest down to local officialdom represented by the scribes. This entire structure placed an intolerable burden of taxation, land dispossession and grinding poverty on the peasants, made worse by religious dogma that blamed their plight on punishment by a vengeful God.

Jesus set out on a deliberate policy of nonviolent resistance and of teaching by demonstration about a loving, merciful God. From preaching sermons so inflammatory that the congregation tried to throw him over a cliff, to deliberately breaking religious rules as publicly as possible, he seems to have gone out of his way to be provocative. He healed the man with the withered hand in front of all his critics instead of doing it quietly round the back of the synagogue; he openly challenged the priestly monopoly on forgiveness; he disappointed the people's apocalyptic expectation of violent vindication by a God of justice by riding calmly into the seat of power on a humble donkey; and then as a climax he caused a major riot, complete with property damage, right at the very centre of the oppressive power structure. No wonder they had to get rid of him.

It is important to note that during all this time, Jesus was carefully, lovingly building up the alternative community, showing through example and teaching how life in communion with a loving God is possible. This, to me, is what the Last Supper is all about. Nothing to do with a sacrificial offering to appease an angry God, but everything to do with building, uniting, strengthening the beloved community for the task ahead.

For this, I believe, is what we are called to do. As believers in a God of love and compassion, we are called to resist all that destroys fullness of life. This is the power that leads my friend Art Laffin to witness week by week at the doors of the Pentagon (the "heart of the empire" as he calls it). This is what leads my friend Angie to work alongside Palestinian villagers despite frequent attempts by the Israeli authorities to prevent her. This is what led hundreds of US citizens to break their government's embargo on Iraq by crowding out the post office with parcels. This is what leads some of us to refuse to pay our taxes towards military purposes. Because the domination system, both political and religious is alive and well in our present day, and we are part of the resistance. At least, I hope we are.

In 2002 at the Big Blockade at Faslane Naval Base, Brian and Jan, warden and deputy warden of Iona Abbey, were among the many who were arrested. They were trying to meet a deadline for the publication of a new worship book for the Abbey, and both agreed to spend their time in the cells thinking and praying about it. This is the affirmation of faith that resulted from their time in the cells:

> We believe that God is present
> In the darkness before dawn;
> In the waiting and the uncertainty
> Where fear and courage join hands,
> Conflict and caring link arms,
> And the sun rises over barbed wire.
> We believe in a with-us God
> Who sits down in our midst
> To share our humanity.
> We affirm a faith
> That takes us beyond the safe place:

Into action, into vulnerability
And into the streets.
We commit ourselves to work for change
And put ourselves on the line:
To bear the responsibility, take risks,
Live powerfully and face humiliation;
To stand with those on the edge;
To choose life
And be used by the Spirit
In God's new community of hope.

(Iona 2001)

It is this kind of conviction and commitment that gives us perfect freedom. If our prayer life, however we interpret it, can put us in touch with the great power for good in the universe, then the good news is about liberation. We have full authority to be different, to be difficult, to swim against the tide, and to live life freely and abundantly.

We are Free and Kept Alive by Hope: Thoughts on Resurrection

Friends often ask me how I have managed to keep on campaigning year after year with no apparent signs of success – indeed all too often the contrary, as the world seems to plunge deeper into despair. I usually reply rather flippantly by describing my work as beating my head against a brick wall hoping to find a rubber brick!

At a more serious level, many people have asked whether I could do work for peace without a spiritual or religious basis. I know, and have a huge respect for, many campaigners who would make no claim to any kind of spiritual motivation for their work (although I might challenge their definition of spiritual), but for myself I know that I could not sustain the work without the support and strength of my faith.

This is where I have an interpretation of the meaning of resurrection which I find helpful. To many, a belief in resurrection is concerned with life after death. For myself, I am not prepared to speculate too much on that. I feel that we make so many good and wonderful connections and relationships during our lives on earth, that it would be a waste for some kind of continuance of beauty and love not to exist, but I am quite content to leave that in trust for the future.

Resurrection, to my mind, seems rather to do with overcoming fear – fear of failure, fear of ridicule, fear of death. "Death, where is thy sting?" is a triumphant shout of defiance to the powers of oppression, that they can do their worst in a physical sense, but ultimately cannot crush the Spirit.

There is a wonderful description of the funeral of Victor Jara of Chile. Victor Jara was a well-known radical and political folk-singer and brilliant guitarist. At the time of the overthrow of Allende's government, Victor was one of thousands imprisoned in the huge stadium in Santiago. He was tortured, his fingers were broken, and eventually he was executed. Despite a heavy military clampdown, thousands defied the authorities and came out on the streets to hold his funeral. Overlooked from machine-gun posts on the roof tops and on street corners, the crowd might have been understandably intimidated, until someone shouted out "Victor Jara – *presente!*"; one after another the names of the dead and disappeared were shouted out, and for each one the crowd shouted *"Presente!"* – here with us.

Another of our Iona Community liturgies calls on the great heroes and heroines of the past in the words, "Columba, stand with us!", "Martin Luther King, stand with us!", "Rosa Parks, stand with us!"; and all our companions in the struggle – stand with us.

And thus the torch of resistance is passed on to us, their successors. On the wall near the spot where Martin Luther King was assassinated there is a plaque which says, "Don't let the dream die".

So what about those times of despair, those desperate times when all our endeavours seem to be futile, when all our hopes lie in ashes and the future seems totally hopeless? It is at this point that holding on to resurrection hope in the midst of disaster becomes a matter of crucial importance.

Jesus' cry of despair from the cross, "My God, my God, why have you forsaken me?" was a cry of deepest anguish that all he had worked for, believed in, hoped for, all the promise of good news, all the dream of justice and a new world, lay in ruins, utterly defeated by the cruel might of the state. Some have interpreted his last words, "It is finished", as a shout of triumph for work completed. Personally I cannot but feel that in that situation he was much more likely to have given a shout of anguished despair.

And yet within a short time, a tiny band of the most unlikely followers emerged from the seeming death of all their hopes and proceeded to turn the world upside down.

It was in December 1982 that 30,000 women had "Embraced the Base" by linking arms around the perimeter of the US air base at Greenham Common, to show their opposition to cruise missiles. The next day, 13 December, many women stayed on to blockade the base. I was one of a group of around 500 blocking the entrance to the so-called Red Gate. There was a huge police presence and some of their handling of us was quite rough, with women being dragged by the hair, having their arms twisted and being kicked in the face. However, the blockade was holding. Suddenly a rumour swept through the crowd, "Here come the riot police." Sure enough, minutes later vans arrived and disgorged hundreds of police equipped with shields and visors. I saw one rolling up his sleeves declaring, "We'll soon clear this lot." Within about five minutes, like a knife through butter, they had broken the blockade and traffic was rolling again to take the workers into the base.

I was sitting at the side of the road in tears, like most of the others, when suddenly, ringing through my head, came the words and the music of Bach's *Magnificat*: "He has scattered the proud in the imagination of their hearts." And I suddenly knew with a sure conviction that although we had been scattered like chaff on this occasion, this was not the end of the road; that some day the proud would indeed be scattered and the mighty cast down.

Eventually cruise missiles did leave Greenham Common and a couple of years ago there was a ceremony of taking down the fence and returning the land to the commons.

This might seem to suggest a contradiction to some of our earlier arguments about God not being "beyond", transcendent, able to pull the strings. Personally I see no contradiction, because the workings of God are within the heart and within the context of events. Someone, somewhere, is moved and inspired to take action and the struggle goes on.

In the middle of Wenceslas Square in Prague there is a monument to Jan Palach, the young student who burned himself to death in protest at the Soviet crushing of the rising. At the time it seemed a useless throwing away of a young life; nothing changed, the Czech uprising was crushed by the Soviet tanks and the world looked on. Now we speak of the later "Velvet Revolution" which liberated Czechoslovakia as a model of nonviolent resistance. When I looked at that monument in Wenceslas Square I began to understand its success. A photograph of Jan Pallach is surrounded by a parapet two or three feet high. At first it looks like stone, but when you bend down to touch it, you realise that it is not stone but the hardened wax of countless hundreds of candles burned over the years.

The important part is the doing, the stepping out in faith. Doing our utmost, to the very limit of our being, and then being free to let go of the result; not to be bound by success, but to hold on to the confidence that the outcome will be taken up by others and the flame continue to burn. Back again to that word "steadfast": we ourselves being steadfast, trusting that others will be steadfast in their turn.

Perhaps a reminder here about the meaning of heroics is in order. We have all looked at the deeds of others and said, "I could never do that". That is not the point. Heroism is not necessarily about great dramatic deeds of daring. We are not called to imitate each other's actions nor to feel disempowered by our failure to be what we are not. We are called to be faithful, to follow our own inner leadings, in our own time, using the particular and special gifts that are unique to each one of us.

But the importance remains in the doing. It involves taking risks, daring to be different from the crowd, keeping in touch constantly with our inner Light, knowing that countless others are doing the same, all making a difference.

Undoubtedly one of the lowest moments of my life was when HMS *Vanguard*, first of Britain's Trident submarines, arrived on the Clyde. Although we had known it was coming for years and had been campaigning vigorously and creatively for just as many years, I don't think anything could have prepared us psychologically for the shock of its reality. Just seeing the huge grey-black bulk being manoeuvred into position at the end of the loch, and realising the full significance of its deadly potential for total annihilation of all that we valued and held dear, was a desperate, heart-stopping moment.

As I have already told, we all launched our little boats as a protest against its progress up the loch. My canoe had been stopped by a boat load of marines, who having informed me that they were saving my life, held firmly on to my craft. I could only sit there in tears watching the inexorable progress of *Vanguard* as it thrust its way up the Gareloch. I had never felt so helpless and powerless in my life. When we came on shore, people gathered round and began singing "We shall overcome". I simply couldn't join them.

Unexpected as it may seem, this for me is the point of resurrection. The point where we have done all we can to the best of our ability, however feeble or seemingly useless, and then we have to hand it over, to let go. Let go of the outcome of one's actions in trust and confidence that they are not in vain, that somewhere in the secret workings of God, a change is taking place.

Because the evidence of history is that change *does* happen – indeed, that is what history is.

Ten Tips for Practical Praying

- ✿ Relax about it and don't worry. Throw away guilt if you find prayer difficult.
- ✿ Think creatively and widely about what prayer might be and find a way that suits you. It could be weeding the garden, drawing mandalas, walking the dog, painting, playing the violin. Choose something that is not technically too difficult, to free up the mind and the imagination.
- ✿ Make a regular time for your prayer activity. Not necessarily daily, although that is helpful, but try to make it regular like brushing your teeth.
- ✿ Make a place for it. No need to mortify the flesh. Find a comfortable corner, a place you like and can return to in imagination when you are not there, and make it your own private spot.
- ✿ Decide whether you want to be part of a group, but make sure the group is compatible – some can lay on an agenda of their own.
- ✿ Tell people that you need space and see that they respect it.
- ✿ Try exploring other groups' ways of praying and go on a retreat or organise your own prayer weekend; e.g. Ignatian, Iona, Key House, Woodbrooke.
- ✿ Follow a study course; e.g. *Hearts and Minds Prepared*, or *Gifts and Discoveries*.
- ✿ Consider prayer an adventure and be prepared to be surprised. Write down your results and any tasks that come up.
- ✿ If you find yourself challenged, find a support group and don't go it alone.

Above all enjoy yourself

Appendices & Bibliography

Appendix 1: *The Iona Community*

Iona Community Vision and Goals

The Iona Community is:

- ∞ an ecumenical movement of men and women from different walks of life and different traditions in the Christian church;
- ∞ committed to the gospel of Jesus Christ, and to following where that leads, even into the unknown;
- ∞ engaged together, and with people of goodwill across the world, in acting, reflecting and praying for justice, peace and the integrity of creation;
- ∞ convinced that the inclusive community we seek must be embodied in the community we practice.

So we share a common discipline of:

- ∞ daily prayer and reading the Bible;
- ∞ mutual accountability for our use of time and money;
- ∞ spending time together;
- ∞ action for justice and peace.

And are, together with our staff, responsible for:

- ∞ our islands residential centres of Iona Abbey, the MacLeod Centre on Iona, and Camas Adventure Centre on the Ross of Mull; and in Glasgow;
- ∞ the administration of the Community;
- ∞ our work with young people;
- ∞ our publishing house, Wild Goose Publications;
- ∞ our association in the revitalising of worship with the Wild Goose Resource Group.

Our History

The Iona Community was founded in Glasgow in 1938 by George MacLeod, minister, visionary and prophetic witness for peace, in the context of the poverty and despair of the Depression. Its original task of rebuilding the monastic ruins of Iona Abbey became a sign of hopeful rebuilding of community in Scotland and beyond. Today, we are about 250 Members, mostly in Britain, and 1500 Associate Members, with 1400 Friends worldwide. Together and apart, "we follow the light we have, and pray for more light".

Our Task

Our task is to discover new ways of living the gospel of Jesus Christ in the world through working for peace and social and environmental justice, rebuilding community and in the renewal of worship.

Justice and Peace Commitment of the Iona Community

We believe:

1. that the Gospel commands us to seek peace founded on justice and that costly reconciliation is at the heart of the Gospel;

2. that work for justice, peace and an equitable society is a matter of extreme urgency;

3. that God has given us partnership as stewards of creation and that we have a responsibility to live in right relationship with the whole of God's creation;

4. that, handled with integrity, creation can provide for the needs of all, but not for the greed which leads to injustice and inequality, and endangers life on earth;

5. that everyone should have the quality and dignity of a full life that requires adequate physical, social and political opportunity, without the oppression of poverty, injustice and fear;

6. that social and political action leading to justice for all people and encouraged by prayer and discussion is a vital work of the Church at all levels;

7. that the use or threatened use of nuclear and other weapons

of mass destruction is theologically and morally indefensible and that opposition to their existence is an imperative of the Christian faith.

As Members and Family Groups we will:

8. engage in forms of political witness and action, prayerfully and thoughtfully, to promote just and peaceful social, political and economic structures;

9. work for a British policy of renunciation of all weapons of mass destruction and for the encouragement of other nations, individually and collectively, to do the same;

10. celebrate human diversity and actively work to combat discrimination on grounds of age, colour, disability, mental wellbeing, differing ability, gender, race, ethnic and cultural background, sexual orientation or religion;

11. work for the establishment of the United Nations as the principal organ of international reconciliation and security, in place of military alliances;

12. support and promote research and education into non-violent ways of achieving justice, peace and a sustainable global society;

13. work for reconciliation within and among nations by international sharing and exchange of experience and people, with particular concern for politically and economically oppressed nations.

Address

Iona Community, 4th Floor, Savoy House, 140 Sauchiehall Street, Glasgow, G2 3DH
e-mail ionacomm@gla.iona.org.uk
website www.iona.org.uk

Appendix 2: *Trident Ploughshares*

Aims

Trident Ploughshares is taking place within the context of an international peace movement which has been actively engaged in nuclear disarmament work ever since the first use of nuclear weapons in Hiroshima and Nagasaki over 50 years ago.

As global citizens we will endeavour to openly, accountably, safely and peacefully disarm the British nuclear weapon system, which is deployed on Trident submarines. **Our acts of disarmament are intended to stop ongoing criminal activity under well-recognised principles of international law.** We will do this as our part of an international citizens' initiative to encourage a nuclear-weapon-free world and an international culture of peace and co-operation.

General Overview of Trident Ploughshares

By January 2001, 175 Ploughshares activists from fifteen different countries, united under an agreed set of nonviolence and safety ground rules, and organised into supportive affinity groups, had undergone a common preparation in order to attempt to disarm the British nuclear Trident system. Each activist signs a Pledge to Prevent Nuclear Crime and a public list of their names is sent to the Government every three months.

Serious and considered dialogue and negotiation is continually offered to the British Government with a set of criteria for nuclear disarmament. If promises of serious and meaningful nuclear disarmament are forthcoming then Trident Ploughshares will stop its active and practical disarmament actions, but meanwhile they will continue.

Trident Ploughshares was launched on 2 May 1998 in Edinburgh, Gent, Gothenburg, Hiroshima and London. To date there have been 2200 arrests, 503 trials, a total of 2184 days spent in prison, and fines imposed (but not necessarily paid) amounting to £72, 819.50. Most actions are "minimum disarmament actions" (eg blockades and fence-cutting), but there have been eight "maximum disarmament actions" of which three were successful. Rachel and Rosie disarmed testing equipment on HMS *Vengeance* in February 1999, Ellen, Ulla and Angie disarmed *Maytime* at Loch Goil in June 1999, and Susan and Martin disarmed a warhead convoy vehicle at RAF Wittering in November 2000.

Trident Ploughshares Pledgers have committed themselves to continual disarmament attempts until the Government commit to disarming Trident themselves.

Address

Trident Ploughshares, 42–46 Bethel Street, Norwich, Norfolk NR2 1NR
e-mail tp2000@gn.apc.org
website www.tridentploughshares.org

Appendix 3 *Some Useful Addresses and Websites*

Amnesty International
119 Rosebery Avenue, London, EC1R 4RE
tel 020 7814 6200
website www.amnesty.org.uk

Campaign Against Arms Trade
11 Goodwin Street, London N4 3HQ
tel 020 7281 0297
website www.caat.org.uk

Campaign for Nuclear Disarmament
162 Holloway Road, London, N7 8DQ
tel 020 7700 2393
website www.cnduk.org

Edinburgh Peace and Justice Centre
St John's Church, Princes Street, Edinburgh EH2 4BJ
tel 0131 229 0993
e-mail peace-justice@btconnect.com

Housmans Bookshop *produces the Peace Diary, which has*
addresses of campaigning organisations around the world
5 Caledonian Road, London N1 9DX
tel 020 7837 4473

Fellowship of Reconciliation
Eirene Centre, The Old Schoolhouse, Clopton, Kettering, NN14 3DZ
tel 01832 720257
website www.gn.apc.org/fore

Iona Community
4th Floor, Savoy House, 140 Sauchiehall Street, Glasgow, G2 3DH
tel 0141 332 6343
website www.iona.org.uk

Iona Abbey and Macleod Centre
Isle of Iona, Argyll, PA76 6SN
tel 01681 700404

Key House *a prayer and retreat centre*
Key Cottage, High Street, Falkland KY15 7BU
tel 01337 857705

Quaker Peace and Social Witness
Friends House, Euston Road, London, NW1 2BJ
tel 020 7663 1000
website www.quaker.org.uk

Scottish CND
15 Barrland Street, Glasgow, G41 1QH
tel 0141 423 1222
website www.dial.pipex.com/cndscot

Scottish Centre for Nonviolence
The Annexe, Scottish Churches House, Dunblane, FK15 0AJ
website www.nonviolence-scotland.org.uk

St Beuno's Ignatian Retreat Centre
St Asaph, Denbighshire, Wales, LL17 0AS
tel 01745 583444
website www.beunos.com

Trident Ploughshares
42–46 Bethel Street, Norwich, NR2 1NR
tel 01324 880744
website www.tridentploughshares.org

Bibliography

Bible. Authorised Version; New Revised Standard Version (New RSV). Oxford University Press, 1995.

Boesak, Allan. *Walking on Thorns: the call to Christian obedience.* Geneva: World Council of Churches, 1984.

Buber, Martin. *I and Thou.* New York: Charles Scribner, 1958. First published as *Ich und Du* in 1923.

Chagnon, J. and Luce, D. (eds). *Of Quiet Courage: Poems of Vietnam.* Indochina Mobile Education Project, 1974.

Christian Faith and Practice in the Experience of the Society of Friends (CFP). London: London Yearly Meeting of the Religious Society of Friends, 1960

Gimblett, Sheriff Margaret. 'Summing up, 21 October 1999: transcript on Trident Ploughshares', www.tridentploughshares .org/article767

Gregg, R. *The Power of Nonviolence.* (2nd rev. ed.) London: James Clarke, 1960.

Hughes, Gerard W. *God of Surprises.* London: Darton, Longman & Todd Ltd, 1987.

The Iona Abbey Worship Book. Glasgow: Wild Goose Publications, 2001. www.ionabooks.com

King, Martin Luther. *Strength to Love.* Glasgow: Collins (Fount Paperbacks), 1984. First published 1963.

Lomax, Eric. *The Railway Man.* London: Jonathan Cape, 1995.

Moltmann, Jürgen. *The Future of Creation.* London: SCM, 1979. First published as *Zukunft der Schöpfung*, 1977.

Nelson-Pallmeyer, Jack. *Jesus Against Christianity: reclaiming the missing Jesus.* Harrisburg, PA: Trinity Press International, 2001.

Quaker Faith and Practice (QFP). London: Yearly Meeting of the Religious Society of Friends in Britain, 1995

Rich, Adrienne. *The Dream of a Common Language, Poems 1974–1977.* New York: W.W. Norton, 1978.